JEWISH — CHRISTIAN RELATIONS

JEWISH-CHRISTIAN RELATIONS

Edited by
Robert Heyer

PAULIST PRESS
NEW YORK, PARAMUS, N.J.

Art and Design: Gloria Ortiz

Photos: Rick Smolan
(except Ch. 1 photo by Paul M. Schrock)

Library of Congress
Catalog Card Number: 75-73

ISBN: 0-8091-1869-6

Published by Paulist Press
Editorial Office: 1865 Broadway, N.Y., N.Y. 10023
Business Office: 400 Sette Drive, Paramus, N.J. 07652

Printed and bound in the United States of America

CONTENTS

ANTI-JUDAISM IS THE LEFT HAND OF CHRISTOLOGY

Paul M. Schrock

Rosemary Radford Ruether

The anti-Semitic legacy of Christian civilization cannot be dealt with either as an accidental or as a peripheral element. Nor can it be dismissed as a legacy from "paganism" or as the product of purely sociological conflicts between the Church and the

Rosemary Ruether is a professor of religion at Howard University and a noted author. In the spring, Harper & Row will publish her *Faith and Fratricide*, a study on the theological source of anti-Semitism.

synagogue. At its root anti-Semitism in Christian civilization springs directly from Christian theological anti-Judaism. It was Christian theology which developed the thesis of the eternal reprobate status of the Jew in history and laid the foundation for the demonic view of the Jews that fanned the flames of popular hatred. This hatred was not only inculcated by Christian preaching and biblical exegesis, but it became incorporated into the structure of both Christian Canon Law and the civil law formed under the Christian Roman emperors, expressed in the Codes of Theodosius (428 A.D.) and Justinian (6th century). The anti-Judaic laws of the Church and the Christian state laid the basis for the inferiorization of the civic and personal status of the Jew in Christian society that lasted until the emancipation of the Jews in the 19th century. In this brief essay I wish to summarize some of the central elements of this theological tradition and how it was translated into the social denigration of the Jew in Christendom.[1]

Theologically anti-Judaism developed as the left hand of Christology. That is to say, anti-Judaism was the negative side of the Christian affirmation that Jesus was the Christ. Christianity claimed the Jewish tradition of messianic hope and believed that Jesus fulfilled that hope. But since the Jewish tradition itself rejected this claim, the Church developed its polemic against the Jews (i.e., the Jewish religious tradition) to explain how the Church could claim to be the fulfillment of a Jewish religious tradition which the Jewish religious tradition itself denied. At the root of this dispute lies an essentially different understanding of the messianic role as this developed in Christianity, in contrast to the Old Testament and Jewish tradition. Judaism looked to the coming of the Messiah as a public, world-historical event which unequivocally overthrew the forces of evil in the world and established the kingdom of God. Originally Chris-

tians also linked Jesus' messianic role intimately to this final salvation of the world. But as this event failed to materialize, Christian theology pushed it off into a vague future— i.e., the "Second Coming"—and reinterpreted Jesus' messianic role in inward and personal ways that bore little relation to what the Jewish tradition had meant by the "coming of the Messiah." Thus an impasse developed between Christianity and Judaism over messianism, since the Christian view of the messianic coming was fundamentally unacceptable to Judaism.

But the real differences between these two views have never really been discussed between Christians and Jews, because at an early stage of development this difference was covered over by communal alienation and mutual polemic. Christianity sought to reconcile its view of the messianic coming with that of the Old Testament (the very term "Old Testament" is itself a Christian anti-Judaic interpretation of the Jewish Scriptures). At the same time Christian exegesis sought to prove that the Jews had ever been apostate from God and their religious leaders spiritually blind and hard of heart, in order to explain the Jewish rejection of the Christian interpretation of the messianic tradition. Christian theology, in effect, set out to prove the rejected status of the Jewish community and the spiritual blindness of its tradition of exegesis and spirituality in order to vindicate the correctness of its own exegesis and its claim to be the rightful heir of Israel's election.

The Christian polemic against Judaism did not stop merely with proving the special guilt of the religious leaders of the Jewish community for the death of Jesus (today recognized to be a dubious thesis). Rather it quickly ramified out into arguments intended to prove the inability of the teachers of this community to read Scripture rightly and the discredited status of Jewish religious law, worship and even their past history back to Moses. In Christian exegesis of the Jewish Scriptures, Jewish history is split down the middle. There is the attempt to prove that there has always existed, in the divine intentionality, a true people of faith who are the rightful heirs of the promise to Abraham, over against a fallen, disobedient people who never obeyed God or heard the prophets and who, from the beginning, rejected and even killed the prophets and so could be expected to reject and even kill the Messiah, the promised redeemer of the prophetic tradition, when he appeared. This comes to be seen as the logical climax of the evil history of the Jewish people. It is the Church which is the true heir to the promise to Abraham. It is the spiritual community of faith, foretold by the prophets, while the "Jews" (that is to say, that religious community that continues to gather around the temple and synagogue and the rabbinic leadership, and which rejects the Church's Christological interpretation of the Jewish Scriptures) were the heir to this evil history of perfidity, apostasy and murder. As a result the Jewish people have been cut off from their divine election. Divine wrath has been poured down on them in the destruction of the temple and the national center in Jerusalem. They have been driven into exile and reprobation until the end of time, when Jesus will return as the Christ and the Jews will finally have to acknowledge their error.

These are the main outlines of the polemic against the Jews as it developed in the exegetical tradition that underlies the New Testament and hardened into a fixed form in the *Adversos Judaeos* tradition in the Church Fathers. Many of the basic themes of this tradition were already set within the New Testament; for example, the ideas that the Jewish people have always killed the prophets and so will kill the Messiah when he comes, as predicted by the prophets; that their worship and religious leaders are discredited; that their teachers are "blind guides"; that their spirituality is hypocrisy and lacks the capacity to save; that the law was given not to save, but to reveal sin; and, finally, that the Jews have lost their election, which has been transferred to the Gentile Church, and that the destruction of Jerusalem is the sign of their present reprobate status. However these arguments were greatly elaborated in the writings of the Church Fathers in the period between the second and fifth centuries in a way that hardened the lines between the two communities.

The themes of the patristic anti-Judaic polemic center around two main theses: (1) the rejection of the Jews and election of the Gentile

Church, and (2) the abrogation of the law. As in the New Testament, the Jewish rejection of the Messiah is read back into the Old Testament as a heritage of evil-doing that culminated in this final act of apostasy. The Jews are said to have always rejected the prophets, refused to hear their message of repentance and to have even killed them. Moreover the Jews are said to be inveterate idol worshipers. Beginning with the golden calf, the Jews turned from God and worshiped idols. God sent the prophets to rebuke this idol worship, but to no avail. This thesis is proved by reading the prophets one-sidedly, forgetting that the context of the prophetic message was, in fact, the acceptance of this message by the Jewish religious tradition! Even worse crimes are hinted at, again using prophetic and psalmic texts out of context. The Jews are said to have been cannibals and to have sacrificed their children to idols. All manner of debauchery, lewdness and immorality are also added to the list of crimes said to characterize the evil character of "the Jews." By the time we reach writers such as St. John Chrysostom in the late fourth century, this picture of the Jews in Christian writings has taken on demonic proportions. The Jews come to be painted as preternatural demonic figures with a superhuman appetite for every depravity of flesh and spirit.

The Mosaic law is said to have been given to the Jews, not as a special mark of election and favor by God, but rather to curb this incorrigible proclivity for idolatry and vice. As the fourth century Church historian Eusebius puts it, "Everything which the Law forbids, they had previously done without restraint" (*Demonstrations of the Gospel,* Bk. 1). Some of the Church Fathers postulate a pre-Mosaic period before the law when patriarchal humanity obeyed God from the heart, guided only by the natural law implanted in the conscience. Christianity is said to have restored this patriarchal era of spiritual obedience. Mosaic religion is therefore painted as an era of fall. The giving of the law comes to represent not a special grace, but a punitive restraint on the special viciousness of the Jews, who are presumed to have picked up their proclivity for idolatry and unnatural vice during their stay in Egypt!

The hermeneutical method for demonstrating this tale of evil Jewish history consists of splitting the right from the left hand of the prophetic message. All the negative descriptions, judgments and threats are taken out of context and read monolithically as descriptive of "the Jews." The positive side of the prophetic message, the traits of repentance, faith and future promise, are said to apply to the future Church. The heroes of the Old Testament become the lineage of the Church, while the Jews are regarded as a people "on probation" who fail the tests and are finally cast off by God. By splitting prophetic judgement from prophetic hope, applying one side to the Jews and the other to the Church, one gains an unrelieved tale of apostasy supposedly characteristic of the

Old Testament people, while depriving the Church of the tradition of prophetic self-criticism. Anti-Judaism and ecclesial triumphalism thus arise as two sides of the same antithesis.

The final crime of this evil history is the killing of the Messiah. Indeed it was to give this "crime" a heritage and "tradition" that Christian apologetics read Jewish history in this manner. As Christology is heightened to the full doctrine of Nicene faith, this comes to be seen not simply as the killing of the final prophet, but as the killing of God, the crime of "deicide," a crime of treason and *lèse majesté* against the sovereign of the universe. For criminals of such a stamp no vituperation is too extreme, as can be seen in the sermons of John Chrysostom who speaks of the Jews continuously as devils, their synagogues as brothels of the devil and the very souls of Jews as dwelling places of demons.

For this final crime the Jews are exiled and their election has been revoked. Their city has been destroyed and their cult place ravished, never to be rebuilt. All their former favor with God and tokens of election have been taken from them. They have been driven into captivity among their enemies, there never to know any cessation of misery until the end of time.

The Fathers are fond of using the mistranslated phrase from Psalm 69:23—"Their back bend thou down always"[2]—to represent this historical status of the Jews since the time of Jesus (see, for example, the trea-tises against the Jews by Hippolytus and by Augustine). The former captivities of the Jews are said to have had limits set by God, and the restorations promised in the Scriptures refer to these former restorations. But this final exile has no limits and is intended by God to last to the end of time. Thus Christian theology took a dogmatic stance which denied the possibility that the Jewish people would ever be restored to their national homeland (a tradition not without significance for present Jewish-Christian misunderstandings over Christian relations to the state of Israel). According to patristic tradition, the Jews are to remain in this status of exile and reprobation until Jesus returns in glory and the Jews are given the final chance to acknowledge their mistake. In this framework, pressure on the Jewish community to convert to Christianity also took on an eschatological significance for Christians, since the mass conversion of the Jews was supposed to signal the approach of the coming of Christ. Even circumcision is said to have been given to the Jews, not as a sign of election, but as a witness to their reprobation that they might be recognized as Jews and prevented from re-entering the city of Jerusalem from which they had been barred after the Jewish wars. Circumcision thus becomes reinterpreted as a kind of "mark of Cain" by which the Jews are to be preserved to the end of time as a wandering reprobate people. The political overtones of this view are evident in the following passage from the 4th century Christian poet Prudentius: "From place to place the homeless Jew wanders in ever shifting exile, since the time when he was torn from the abode of his fathers and has been suffering the penalty for murder and having stained his hands with the blood of Christ whom he denied, paying the price of sin. . . . This noble race (is) . . . scattered and enslaved. . . . It is in captivity under the younger faith. . . . A race that was formerly unfaithful confesses Christ (the Gentiles) and triumphs. But that which denied Christ is conquered and subdued and has fallen into the hands of masters who keep the faith" (*Apotheosis*, 541-550).

This anti-Judaic tradition grew into a fixed standpoint between the second and fourth centuries. It was repeated over and over again in every Christian sermon, biblical commentary or theological treatise that touched on the Jews. And since Christians claimed Jewish Scriptures as their own and understood themselves as the heirs of the election of Israel, it was difficult to preach or teach anything without touching on the Jews in some way. Then, in the fourth century, the Church was transformed from a persecuted sect to the established religion of the empire. By 380 A.D. orthodox Christianity had become the exclusive faith of all citizens of this empire. The faith and practice of pagans and heretics was proscribed by law. Their temples and churches were destroyed or confiscated. Toward the Jews, however, the attitude was more complicated. The Jews had gained a protected status in Roman law. They were Roman citizens at

this time, and their right to worship and govern their communities internally by Jewish law was guaranteed. Moreover, although Christian theology decreed misery for the Jews, it did not decree extermination. Indeed it demanded the on-going existence of the Jews, although in a status of reprobation, as the continuing witness to the triumph of the Church and the final witness to Christ at the end of time. Thus the paradox of the Church's attitude to the Jews was that it was simultaneously committed to the preservation of the Jews and, at the same time, to making them exhibit externally the marks of their reprobation. It was out of this contradiction that the tragic history of the Jews in Christian society was to flow.

By the fourth century the Christian view of the Jews began to be enacted into law by the Christian emperors. The basic principle of this legislation was that the Jews should be allowed the bare minimum of continued right to worship, but that they should have no honor in Christian society and should be removed from any possibility of holding authority over Christians. The Jews were forbidden from circumcizing and then from owning slaves. Since Jewish families incorporated their servants into their households religiously, this was intended to remove a potent source of influence of Jews over Christians (remembering that Christians themselves had risen from the slave class). Severe laws were passed forbidding Jews from converting Christians to Judaism, and also against any interference with the

Church's conversion of Jews to Christianity. Although Jews were allowed to worship, laws forbade them from building new synagogues or repairing old ones. By the fifth century the public recognition of the Jewish patriarch and his delegates was withdrawn, a severe blow to the ability of Judaism to communicate throughout the Diaspora. Jews were forbidden from holding any civil or military office and barred from the *cursus honorum* of the state. They could not be judges or represent themselves in court. The idea that a Jew might hold authority over a Christian is termed in one law in the Theodosian canon "an insult to our faith." The laws bristle with theologically loaded epithets which condemn the Jews as a vicious people, and the synagogue is even referred to in one law as a "brothel" (*C. Th.* 16/8/1). Since agriculture and industry were carried out by slaves (later serfs), exclusion from holding slaves eliminated Jews from agriculture and large industry. In addition to these civil laws the Church added laws condemning intermarriage or religious fraternization of any kind between Jews and Christians. The Church also incorporated the civil anti-Judaic laws into ecclesiastical codes and passed these down to the Germanic states that succeeded the Western Roman empire.

By the late fourth century this official persecution of the Jews was supplemented by outbreaks of popular violence against the Jews in the form of synagogue burnings, expulsions and forced baptisms. The emperors sought to hold the line against these popular excesses, usually led by fanatical monks. But bishops often justified this violence and rebuked the emperor when he sought reparations for the Jewish community (see the epistles of St. Ambrose, 40 and 41). Thus through a combination of official inferiorization from the Church and Christian state and hatred whipped up by popular preachers, the ghetto was gradually shaped around the Jewish community in Christendom until practices such as the "Jewish badge" and the ghetto walls became institutions by the late Middle Ages. This status of the Jew as a person without honor or civil rights in Christian society was to last until modern times and was swept away in Eastern Europe only by the Nazi Holocaust itself!

The translation of theological vituperation into popular hatred was by no means automatic. Although popular pogroms took place in the fourth and fifth centuries in Syria and Alexandria, where communal tension between Jews and other groups could be fanned into flames by the new theological views, many other Christians continue to fraternize with the Jewish community and to regard Jewish observances as their own. Large groups of Judaizers in Antioch in the late fourth century continued to frequent the synagogue, especially on high holidays. This fact provided the basis for John Chrysostom's eight vitriolic sermons against the Jews preached at the time of the high holidays. In Byzantine society Jews were strictly reduced to a low social and economic status and official clerical vituperation against them alternated with imperial efforts at forced baptisms. But the tradition of intense popular hatred never developed. This seems to have been partly due to the fact that theological-legal anti-Semitism was never translated into economic terms.

In the West, however, where the city and the money economy failed, the fact that the Jews were the one group that could maintain contact between the Christian West and the trade route of the East, held by the Muslims, made the Jews the catalysts to Western economic revival. Jews also played a key role in the redevelopment of the money economy. But these roles, when combined with the Church's view of the Jews as reprobate and its attempt to confine them to a status without authority in Christian society, resulted in a structuring of the Jewish community into a peculiar economic role. The Jews were forbidden the normal range of economic possibilities. They could be neither farmers nor industrialists (being excluded from the guilds).

Their role as merchants was largely expropriated by the Christians at the time of the crusades. Thus the Jews became the moneylenders (not the only moneylenders by any means; the Italians and others were more than their rivals) for Christian princes. This placed the Jews in the position of living by their wits as economic innovators, while being forced to function simultaneously as the economic agents and the economic scapegoats

for the European ruling class. The financial success of an elite group of Jews was transferred to the coffers of princes, while the financial failure of the princes' policies generated a hatred which was transferred to the Jewish community. It was this combination of theological vituperation, legal-social inferiorization and economic scapegoating that created a worsening image of the Jew in the Middle Ages. At the time of the Crusades, mass popular massacres broke out against the Jews. These events taught the people that the Jewish community, although officially protected by the princes, was actually an easy mark for any mob. Once this lesson had been learned, popular violence against the Jews at times of social crisis never ceased. New myths, such as the stories that Jews killed Christian children and drank their blood on Passover, violated Christian sacraments and poisoned wells, were created to excuse these outbreaks and to foment new ones. By the late Middle Ages the Jew had been transformed into a full-blown devil in Christian popular mythology, complete with horns, a tail and a peculiar stench.

The Christian theological doctrine that the Jew was reprobate in history to the end of time thus translated itself into a practice of social denigration to "prove" this status or reprobation through the outward evidence of social misery. This, in turn, interacted with social and economic factors, until it became transformed into what we must now recognize to be a state of *mass paranoia* toward the Jewish community in Christian

8

popular culture. If the misery of the Jew is necessary to prove his reprobate status and the triumph of the Church, it follows then that any social prospering of the Jew in Christian society or any power he accrues over Christians will be regarded as an affront to Christian society and an implicit attack on Christian faith. It was this mass paranoia that flourished in rampant form in the late Middle Ages and lasted into the age of the ghetto. This was just beginning to dissipate in the 19th and early 20th centuries throughout Western and then in Eastern Europe, when it was revived by Nazism as a tool for doctrines which had little to do with Christian faith!

---

1. This essay will summarize material developed at length in a recently completed book on the theological sources of anti-Semitism, entitled *Faith and Fratricide*, to be published in the spring of 1974 by Harper and Row, with an introduction by Father Gregory Baum, O.S.A.

2. The Hebrew reads "Let their loins tremble continuously." It was mistranslated in the Septuagint Greek text used by Christian writers.

MAJOR ISSUES IN THE JEWISH/CHRISTIAN SITUATION TODAY

Marc H. Tanenbaum

In the first century, Rabbi Hillel, a contemporary of Jesus of Nazareth, was asked by a pagan to instruct him

Rabbi Tanenbaum is National Inter-Religious Affairs Director of the American Jewish Committee and is widely regarded as a leading figure in the advancement of Jewish-Christian understanding. He was the only rabbi present at Vatican Council during the deliberations that led to the adoption of the Conciliar Declaration on Non-Christian Religions. Rabbi Tannenbaum is presently co-secretary of a joint Vatican-International Jewish Committee and of a similar liaison body with the World Catholic Conference.

about the entire Torah while standing on one foot. Being asked to write an article of about 2,000 words on the world of Catholic-Jewish relations involves something of the same order of *chutzpah* (impertinence) and hazard of distortion. Hillel's reply has become a classic model not only of epigrammatic rabbinic wisdom, but of literary brevity as well. "That which is hateful to you," Hillel instructed the pagan, "do not inflict on your fellow human being. All the rest is commentary." No 2,000 words about anything could improve very much on that insight!

But if I cannot improve on Hillel's wisdom, I will defer to him and borrow from his method. If I were asked therefore to summarize the present state of Catholic-Jewish relations, the generalization which keeps coming to mind is that "Catholics and Jews are out of phase." And now let me try to explain, not on one foot, but in some 2,000 words, which in themselves are inadequate when you consider seriously the intense complexity of both the Catholic and Jewish commuinities and traditions.

The Roman Catholic and Jewish communities possess both universal and national religious-ethnic dimensions, and in these senses they have very much in common. They are not simply creedal fellowships, but have rich social substance in which their religious and moral ideals and values are incarnated in the very lives of their peoples. When Vatican Council II shifted the metaphor of Catholic self-understanding from the "mystical body of Christ" to "the pilgrim Church" and the "people of God," those reformulations were instantly understandable to Jewish theologians. Those reconceptualizations were essentially biblical, and forgive the triumphalism, essentially Jewish. Those Catholic affirmations have equivalencies in traditional Jewish categories of self-definition: by divine action at Sinai, the Jews emerged into history as a covenanted people, a "kingdom of priests and a holy nation" obligated to carry out a task of messianic redemption in the world until the coming of the kingdom. Thus, from their very origins Jews have understood themselves as "a holy people of God" on pilgrimage. That growing commonality in the biblical world-view is decisive for understanding everything else that is happening between Catholics and Jews!

As human societies with universal and national aspects, Catholics and Jews have both "foreign" and "domestic" agendas. Each of these agendas reflects the life interests of our respective peoples, interests of survival and continuity, and the time is past due for either Catholics or Jews to feel apologetic or defensive about articulating or pressing for the realization of their legitimate group interests. But shaped by substantially different historical experiences, these "foreign" and "domestic" agendas are in some ways "out of phase" and it is important that we try to understand how we got this way, and what might be done to synchronize these interests where humanly possible. And if we cannot synchronize interests where differences of principle or faith are involved, at the very least we should try to understand the real reasons behind the different positions, and learn how to respect the difference, rather than deal with the other through caricatures and stereotypes which are a violation of truth, justice, and charity.

I begin with the "Jewish agenda" which, for obvious reasons, I know best. Both the "foreign" and "domestic" sides of the Jewish agenda are determined decisively by the two watershed events of contemporary Jewish life—the Nazi Holocaust and the rebirth of the state of Israel. Nazi Germany's mass slaughter of six million Jewish men, women, and children destroyed one-third of the body of the Jewish people. Every Jewish person born in the shadow of Dachau and Auschwitz has learned from that trauma at least three permanent, universal lessons:

First, when your enemy says he is going to destroy you, you take him with absolute seriousness. In Germany in the 1930's, many Jews, inured by their middle class comforts and deceived about the permanence of sin and evil by German *kultur* and *gemutlichkeit,* dismissed Hitler as "a monkey" and as "insane." Jews can no longer afford such delusions and faulty diagnosis.

Second, Jews can no longer tolerate for a moment the luxury of standing by while the blood of their brothers and sisters cries out from the earth. That is why Jews in such disproportionately large numbers marched in Selma and in the civil rights march on Washington; that is why they also joined with Catholics and Protestants in seeking to bring relief for the victims of massacres in the Nigerian-Biafran civil conflict. These were in many ways acts of delayed atonement for the sin of spectatorship during the Nazi genocide when there were few Jewish marches on Berlin and on Washington which could have made some difference; and even if not, there was a moral obligation to try to make a difference that was faulted.

Third, the fact that in our lifetime two out of five Jewish lives were destroyed has filled every Jewish life with heightened value and preciousness. Indeed, it has heightened the Jewish appreciation of the dignity and infinite worth of every human life, but in all candor there is a special intensity in the value attached to a Jewish life. For Jews are a minority people, and the very survival of this people depends on the preservation of "a critical mass" of Jewish persons who can make the sustaining of Jewishness and Judaism meaningful and worthwhile.

These three "lessons"—among others —inform critically the consciousness of the vast majority of Jews today. The overwhelming and unprecedented response of American and world Jewry in solidarity with Israel when attacked by unprovoked Arab aggression on Yom Kippur, the Day of Atonement, cannot be understood apart from these lessons of recent Jewish history. Spiritually, psychologically and existentially, the Jewish people simply cannot afford another single attempt by Arab leaders or anyone else at their "final solution" of the Jewish problem through aggression and mass destruction. Virtually every Jewish person in the world—whether religious, agnostic, or atheist—knew in his or her bones that the destruction of Israel, God forbid, would be the lethal blow that would end all meaning for the Jewish presence in history. Auschwitz epitomized the total vulnerability of Jews as defenseless victims in the scenario wrought demonically by others. Israel, the resurrection of Jews after their death, signified that for the first time in 2,000 years Jews finally were restored to mastery over their own fate and destiny. The universal determination of the Jewish people to try to preserve Israel against attack and aggression meant nothing less, symbolically and actually, than a supreme effort to close once and for always the Auschwitz chapter in Jewish history, with its nightmare images of Jews perennially led as victim sheep to the slaughter.

Animating these human and historical considerations has been the powerful spiritual and moral motif of Judaism which affirms that "he who saves one human life" is regarded as if "he had saved an entire world." Thus, sacrificial giving to the United Jewish Appeal, 35,000 young Jews volunteering their services for kibbutzim and other non-military services, and the giving of blood in vast quantities were all part of acting out the supreme *mitzvah* (religious commandment)—saving life.

On the graph of Jewish priorities, therefore, "foreign" concerns have predominated since the end of the Second World War. In addition to the massive undertaking of saving Jewish refugees from the wreckage of Nazi Germany, and of helping to build a safe haven in Israel, the foreign agendum of Jewry has been preoccupied with concerns for assuring the human rights of the three million Jews in the Soviet Union, with the oppressed and persecuted Jews in Arab countries, especially in Syria and Iraq, and with combatting the massive anti-Israel and anti-Semitic propaganda waged on every continent by the Arab countries and the Communist nations, led by the Soviet Union.

These inescapable "foreign" obligations of preserving as many lives as humanly possible have in many ways overwhelmed the "domestic" needs of American Jewish life. And there are plenty of problems of Jewish survival, continuity, and renewal in America. The impact of the "American way of life"—its powerful assimilative forces, common culture, paganism, hedonism, consumerism, self-indulgence—is having the same corrosive effects on Jewish traditions, group loyalties, and religious indifferentism and relativism as it is on the Catholic community. The most pressing issues on the "domestic" Jewish agendum are those which deal with strengthening the religious and cultural identity of Jews, especially our youth: shoring up Jewish family life which is beginning to erode under the impact of mobility, intermarriage, and zero population growth; enhancing the role of women in the synagogue and Jewish community life; making Jewish education more relevant to the ethical and value needs of our people; reinvigorating synagogue liturgy and ritual in ways that make connections between the tradition and the real needs of our people today.

During recent years, as I have observed relationships between Catholics and Jews, members of the Jewish community have approached their Catholic friends and neighbors for support of causes on the Jewish "foreign" agendum, and here is where the "out of phase" awareness begins to register. There is a Catholic "foreign" and "domestic" agendum that is frequently not well known by Jews.

My impression is that most Catholics are content to leave "foreign" questions to the disposition of the Pope, the Holy See, the national Catholic hierarchy, or the impressive Catholic relief and welfare agencies. Except for the vigorous public anti-war activity of Catholic left groups, mainstream Catholics seem to be far more concerned about "domestic" issues involving personal faith and family life. The intensity of passion and conviction that many Jews exercise over the welfare and security of their brothers and sisters in Israel, the Soviet Union, and the Arab countries finds its parallel in similar intensity of Catholic feelings invested in right-to-life issues—abortion, birth control, involuntary sterilization, and euthanasia. The social dimension of parish Catholic concern seems to be located mainly in such issues of public morality as censorship and combating pornography.

An almost weird kind of "parallel play" seems to be developing between Catholics and Jews on the neighborhood level, and I worry about it. Increasingly, I am inclined to believe that it is not good for the "wholeness" of either Catholic or Jewish morality or spirituality for such "out of phaseness" to continue without correction.

Surely it does not advance the cause of seeking to preserve the dignity of the human person created in the image of God for the right-to-life issues to have become publicly identified as solely a "Catholic" issue, allegedly being imposed on the public by "Catholic power." In fact, the right-to-life issues are supremely issues of biblical morality, and it would have far better served our common spiritual purposes had Catholics, Jews, and Protestants found a way very early in the debate to clear a common ground. The Catholic Church and the Catholic people are to be applauded for having raised to public consciousness the centrality of the dignity of human life issue, but their strategy for building a domestic coalition leaves much to be desired. It is not too late to try to win broad support and understanding for these crucial spiritual and moral issues, and I for one propose to do what I can to bring Jews, Catholics, and others together in alliance for preventing the further erosion of the divine image of God in man.

Similarly, it is not good for the "wholeness" of the Jewish spirit and psyche for Jews to find themselves struggling almost alone for the human rights of Jews in the Soviet Union or for the right of the people and state of Israel to live a peaceful existence with secure, defensible borders. While it is now self-evident that in the pluralism of America, and of the world community, every religious-ethnic community has its own agendum and its own legitimate priorities for which the group itself is expected to be the foremost advocate, for the group to become the sole advocate of the cause invariably casts upon it the cloud of marginality.

I have not the slightest hesitation in saying that had not the Jews of America and elsewhere committed themselves heart and soul to the cause of emigration of Soviet Jews, very few of the 70,000 who were allowed to leave since 1971 would have been liberated. At the same time, the cause of the human rights of Soviet Jews is the identical cause of the human rights of Catholics in Russia, Lithuania, Poland, Latvia, and elsewhere. Jews, Catholics, Baptists and others have very similar problems in Russia and elsewhere in terms of overcoming restrictions that prevent religious education of children, and the conducting of a significant religious life in houses of worship and homes. What great spiritual and political power could be released if Catholics were to join their Jewish neighbors in national and international efforts to compel the Communist countries to conform to the human rights obligations they committed themselves to when they signed the United Nations Charter! It is not enough to leave this to the Holy See, in my judgment. American Catholics, precisely because they are Americans, have an enormous leverage to exercise at this moment in history precisely because the Soviet Union is desperate for American wheat, trade, and technology. No one should underestimate the impact that George Meany of the AFL-CIO and Thomas Gleason of the Maritime Union had in prodding the Soviet Union to play a constructive role in helping bring about a ceasefire in the Middle East when they announced that longshoremen simply would refuse to load the wheat bought by the Soviet Union unless the Russians stopped arming and goading Arab nations to war against Israel. Similar actions in support of the human rights of Catholics, Jews, and other deprived communities in the Soviet Union might produce interesting results not otherwise obtained.

The right to life issue on the domestic agendum of Catholics, and the Soviet Jewry and Israel issues on the foreign agendum of Jews, are simply illustrative of the need to find more effective ways for synchronizing the priority issues of both communities and of replacing much unnecessary polarization by mutual understanding and mutual support. Both Jews and Catholics have got to find a constructive way of meeting the educational needs of their children in non-public schools. The quality education of nearly six million children in parochial and all-day schools is first and foremost an American education issue, rather than a religious issue. If we can send Skylabs to the moon, we certainly must have enough ingenuity to find a formula for aiding our school children without violating the Constitution.

Jews and Catholics have a vital stake in seeking to overcome the widespread religious illiteracy in America, and the counterculture of paganism and hedonism which threatens all the religiously-based values of self-restraint, civility, and respect for the rights of others. When a society tolerates the blasphemy and crude anti-Semitism of *Jesus Christ Superstar* on the grounds that it is "entertainment," it is virtually inevitable that the next step will be encouragement to produce the Danish film on "The Erotic Life of Jesus." Catholics and Jews must stop tilting at windmills, and must together create effective mechanisms to halt the further erosion of religious and ethical disciplines and norms in our society.

And obviously there are other issues which should be calling Catholics and Jews together—America's national priorities of overcoming poverty, providing jobs, housing, education, improved courts of justice, prison reform, health care, aid to the elderly, affirmative action for the disadvantaged, etc. There are also the more elusive but nonetheless significant questions for theologians, scholars, and clergy to engage in together—the moral and ethical challenges of biomedical research which threatens to make man in the image of man rather than in the image of God; the laissez faire model of doing science and technology which is leading to such devastating corruption and pollution of the environment. Catholics and Jews must begin to play some effective role in the decision-making process in these areas which shape

the life of all of us.

How to go about it? I suggest that the time is ripe for Catholics and Jews to begin organizing national, regional, and local "Catholic-Jewish Agenda Meetings" that would enable each group to take inventory in a careful, precise way of all the problems and issues that are of real concern to each community and to place these on a common table for reciprocal consideration.

By replacing vague impressions and stereotyped notions and images about what it is that genuinely concerns our respective communities, and by working out joint and parallel approaches to our common religious and societal problems, we will have gone a long way to implementing the spirit of the Vatican Council *Declaration on Non-Christian Religions* which called for "mutual knowledge and reciprocal respect."

THE RELIGIOUS SIGNIFICANCE OF ISRAEL:

A Christian Perspective

Eva Fleischner

The Christian theologian who tries to explore the religious significance of Israel today—by "today" I mean the past 25 years—starts from scratch as far as his own tradition is concerned. From the late first century C.E. until 1948 there was no Jewish state, so that Christianity did not have to try

Eva Fleischner, Associate Professor of Religion at Montclair State College, where she teaches a Seminar on *The Holocaust*. She is on of the original members of Christians' Concern for Israel. This article was written before the outbreak of the "Yom Kippur War."

to grapple with its significance. It did, however, have plenty of grappling to do with the meaning of the Jewish people. And part of the tradition that emerged from this theological effort was that there never would be a Jewish state again: that homelessness, landlessness until the end of time, were part of the very nature of Judaism—God-willed, God-imposed (albeit through human instruments, who turned out by and large to be Christian instruments), a sign of the reprobation of the Jewish people, part of their punishment for rejecting and crucifying the Messiah.

This tradition has been cracked wide open by recent historical events. However contradictory to traditional Christian teaching the state of Israel may appear, it exists; it is a fact of life. It has survived the first quarter of a century of its precarious existence, and gives every indication of continued survival.

Not only, then, do we start from scratch in attempting to probe the religious significance of Israel, but we have to scrap our traditional teaching about Judaism, which allowed no room for the state's existence. If ever there was an example of history forcing the hand of theology, here it is.

The People and the Land

Where, in this no-man's land in which we currently find ourselves (I use this phrase fully aware of the pioneering work which has been done these past 15 years by some Christian scholars), shall we look for help in working out that new Christian perspective which is urgently needed? I use the phrase "urgently needed" advisedly. We Christians need it because an understanding of Judaism is essential to our own self-understanding, and there can be no understanding of Judaism today without some understanding of the state of Israel. Where, then, shall we look?

Here we need not start from scratch. I believe that our starting point— perhaps no more than that, but at least that—must be the meaning Israel has for the Jew. Unless we

start there, unless we take Jewish self-understanding, of which Israel is a major component, seriously, we shall continue to make our own theological constructs in which Jews fail to recognize themselves; we shall continue to pontificate, to define "the other" in our own terms. This is to reduce him to an object, to deprive him of that basic human right to define himself. It is precisely what Hitler did. Not only does the Jew have that right, like every other man, but we have much to learn from the way in which he sees himself. Moreover, the Jewish understanding of Israel is grounded in those Scriptures which for the Christian too are the Word of God.

In the history of no other people has the land been so intimately interwoven with its destiny, dreams, faith and hope. If it is true that the Jewish people survived for 1,900 years without a land—an historical phenomenon unparalleled to my knowledge— it is also true that the vision of the land, the dream of the return, of the in-gathering, expressed year after year at the closing of the Seder, "Next year in Jerusalem," helped the people survive. No man can survive without hope, and Jewish hope was epitomized in the hope of the return, the faith that, to quote Psalm 147, "The Lord rebuilds Jerusalem, the dispersed of Israel he gathers. He heals the broken-hearted, he binds up their wounds." Abraham Heschel's book, *Israel, An Echo of Eternity,* conveys the almost mystical meaning which Israel and its heart, the city of Jerusalem, still have for Jews today: "Jerusalem is more than a place in space of a memorial to the past. Jerusalem is a prelude, anticipation of days to come. . . . It is not our memory, our past, that ties us to the land. It is our future. . . . Spiritually, I am a native of Jerusalem. I have prayed here all my life. My hopes have their home in these hills. . . . Jerusalem is never at the end of the road. She is the city where waiting for God was born."1

God Is Faithful

The destruction of Jerusalem in 70 C.E., and still more completely in 135 C.E., was interpreted by the early Church as evidence of the rejection of the Jewish people. The covenant God had once made with them was broken, no longer in force, superseded by a new covenant, made with a new people of God, the Church. The original people of God was people of God no longer. It should, logically, have disappeared. But the Jewish people did not disappear. On the contrary, Judaism brought forth, at the moment of its greatest crisis, new and viable forms of life and worship, the creativity of which Christian scholars have only recently begun to acknowledge, even to admire. Christianity solved the problem of the stubborn, embarrassing, continued existence of the Jews by evolving over a period of some 300 years what Jules Isaac has called the "Teaching of Contempt":2 the Jew continues to live, yes, until the end of time (which, incidentally, precludes a Christian "final solution"), but his existence has a purely negative meaning. He carried the mark of Cain on his forehead, is a symbol of

hard-heartedness and faithlessness, and must expiate his sin until the end of time by being deprived of a normal human existence.

It is not my intention here to go into the teaching of contempt, or to delineate the incalculable harm and suffering it has brought upon the Jewish people. Yet I cannot but refer to it here, for at least two reasons:

First, because the rebirth of a Jewish state has put an end to it, hopefully once and for all (although efforts to revive it, as we shall see, are not yet, alas, a thing of the past). The existence of the state of Israel can become a powerful tool in the Christian theological effort to re-examine the meaning and destiny of the Jewish people. It can help us realize that God did not abrogate his covenant with Israel; that the Jews are still his people, beloved and cherished; that his comforting words spoken to them during their first exile long ago through Second Isaiah have been vindicated, not only at that time in the return to their homeland, but down through the ages, and once again in our century: "Thus says the Lord who created you, O Jacob, and formed you, O Israel: Fear not, for I have redeemed you; I have called you by name: you are mine. When you pass through the water I shall be with you; in the rivers you shall not drown; when you walk through fire you shall not be burned; the flames shall not consume you. . . . For I am the Lord, your God, the Holy One of Israel, your Savior. . . . Fear not, for I am with you. From the east I will bring back your descendants, from the west I will gather you. I will say to the north: Give them up! and to the south: Hold not back! Bring back my sons from afar, and my daughters from the ends of the earth" (Is. 43:1-3, 5-7).

This is surely part of the religious significance of Israel for the Christian today: God is faithful; he does not repent of the promises once made. St. Paul said it long ago in Romans 9-11, but these words of his were not heard or understood by Christians through the centuries.

Zionism

My second reason for mentioning the teaching of contempt is that it belongs to the historical background against which the state of Israel must be seen.

The state of Israel is the realization of the dream of Zionism—Zionism understood not as that fundamental, age-old longing for the return to Zion already referred to, but as the 19th-century political movement which made its objective the establishment of a Jewish homeland. While Theodor Herzl was not the founder of Zionism—the idea antedates him—he gave it a new urgency and drive, and is rightly venerated today as the founder of the state of Israel.

Zionism, and Herzl's efforts in particular, were a reaction against the recurring anti-Semitism of 19th-century Europe and the slowly dawning realization of the Jew that despite the French Revolution and emancipation

he still has not obtained full citizenship; or that, where he has obtained it, e.g., in France, it is a fragile right at best, which can be taken away at any time. Herzl might never have become Herzl had he not "by chance" been present in Paris at the trial of Dreyfus—a trial which was the climax of a lengthy, carefully planned, vicious hate campaign against the Jews, spearheaded by the Catholic Drumont and strongly supported by the French Catholic Right. It may be said, therefore, that Christian anti-Semitism played a role in the emergence of Zionism, hence in the eventual emergence of Israel.

The Holocaust

The immediately historical backdrop for the state of Israel is the Holocaust. Indeed, the two events are so closely related historically, religiously and psychologically that the state cannot be understood without the catastrophe that preceded it—a catastrophe so great that Jewish tradition gives it the name "churban," which until then has been reserved for the destruction of the Second Temple.

Yet our generation has known not only the Holocaust, but also the rebirth of a Jewish homeland—a rebirth all the more extraordinary because it occurred a mere three years after the Holocaust: May 1945— May 1948. For the survivors, for many Jews everywhere, it was indeed as though the vision of Ezekiel 37 had come true.

I am well aware of the pitfalls of interpreting history in theological terms, as though we knew "the mind of the Lord or had been his counselor" (Isaiah), or, in the words of Jesus, as though we know "the hour which no one knows but the Father, not even the Son." Yet it is difficult to disagree with Heschel's statement that "Israel enables us to bear the agony of Auschwitz without radical despair, to sense a ray of God's radiance in the jungles of history."[3]

Two overwhelming experiences in one generation, contradictory to each other, contradictory within themselves, but of a scope so as to threaten, or assure, the survival and viability of Israel's exodus experience.[4] I am convinced that no Christian who has not tried to penetrate at least the outskirts of the "kingdom of night," as Elie Wiesel calls it, can understand the state of Israel. The Holocaust is still present as an undercurrent in Israeli life everywhere today, and no doubt will continue to be as long as there are any survivors left. The new state saw as its primary task to be a haven of refuge for the survivors, for Jews everywhere. Auschwitz and Israel are linked in an unbreakable chain, even though nothing, not even the rebirth of the state, can make up for the death of 6,000,000. But if they cannot be brought back to life, the survivors and their children can live, must live.

Let me now turn to consider some elements that may go into a new Christian perspective concerning the state of Israel.

1. Whatever reservations the Chris-

tian may have about the situation in the Middle East—which is in many respects ambiguous and painful—I believe that we must endorse Israel's right to exist. In Psalm 84 we read, "Even the sparrow finds a home, the swallow a nest in which she puts her young." But for 1,900 years the Jew had no home, no place where he could be safe, among his own. One is tempted to interpret Jesus' words, "The Son of Man has nowhere to lay his head," as applying in a unique manner to Jesus' own people. Never has this been more true than in our century, during the Holocaust, when doors remained closed everywhere, when houses, cities, hills and valleys, where so many mothers could have hidden their children from the gas chambers, remained deaf to the cry of anguish. The Jews were trapped.[5]

Israel not only has a right to the land but, after Auschwitz, needs the land—as never before perhaps. Needs it in order to keep faith in God, faith in man. No doubt the UN sensed something of this when it agreed in 1948 to the establishment of the state. Some maintain that it was a way for the nations of the world to clear their consciences of the shared guilt of the Holocaust. This may well be true. But the initial gesture of support is not enough; we must continue to affirm Israel's right to live. The graves do not yield their dead. But Israel makes it possible for the living to live their lives as Jews in freedom and dignity, without shame or fear—the Jews of the Diaspora as much as the Jews of Israel, thanks to Israel, which for Jews everywhere is the

21

symbol of freedom and security and pride today.

2. When I speak of the Christian's duty to support Israel's right to live, I do not mean that this support should be blind or uncritical. Israel needs criticism in order to live up to the high ideal not only of its prophetic tradition, but of its Zionist founders: to be a haven of refuge for the oppressed, a light to the nations. But here we Christians find ourselves caught in a bind. Do we have the right to tell Israel what to do, how to act? In the name of what have we earned that right? I will not say we have forfeited it, because, given the history between us, a history of hostility almost from the beginning, we Christians have never had this right. We have yet to win it, and I believe we can win it. My personal experience gives me that hope. On rare occasions I have been able to voice certain reservations about Israel to my closest Jewish friends, because they had come to trust me, they knew I cared deeply. Therefore my criticism was no longer that of an "outsider" which can only wound, no matter whether it contains truth or not.

3. This brings me to what may well be the major, and perhaps the only, contribution Christians today can make to the current political crisis: we must do everything in our power to foster a climate of trust, in which we may have the freedom to be constructively critical, but—more important—in which Jews will feel free to voice criticism, that self-criticism, that criticism of the community from within, which has been typical of Judaism throughout its history. We know that there is growing self-criticism within Israel today, even among some American Jews. Yet to the outside world Jews present a united front. No wonder, since that world so readily condemns them no matter what they do—whether they "let themselves be led as sheep to the slaughter," or whether they win wars with lightning rapidity. Here Christians could play a key role. Let us live up to the challenge of Jesus; let us become peacemakers, reconcilers. But we shall be accepted as such only if we are trusted. And we shall be trusted only if we shed our ancient and deep-rooted prejudices and begin to identify with the Jewish people, to the point where, if another Hitler comes, we would be ready to share their fate. A few, a very few Christians did just that 30 years ago. The majority stood by silently, in apathy, even glad that Hitler was realizing their secret wish.

4. If all-out support of the Palestinians is often anti-Semitism under a nobler name, I believe that an absolutizing of Israel can also be dangerous, whether on the Jewish or Christian side. This point is closely related to the remarks made earlier about the need for criticism—criticism from within above all, but also from without, provided it arises from sympathy and concern. While for me, as a believing Christian who cares deeply about the destiny of the Jews— hence of Israel—the birth of the state is indeed one link in the chain of God's saving acts, I do not share the

view of those who see Israel in terms of messianic fulfillment. Even among Jews their number is small. Surely we have not yet reached that era when "men into ploughshares turn their swords, nations shall wage war no more." To absolutize Israel is no better than to absolutize Christianity or the Church. The messianic horizon lies still in the future, and must not prematurely be transferred into the here and now. Who can understand this better than Jews? For 2,000 years they have refused to say that the kingdom of God has come, because all is not yet right with the world. Rosemary Ruether speaks of Israel as "a liberating break-through experience *vis à vis* the terrible experience of Jewry in the Christian Exile. But its present reality testifies that it is not the final redemptive messianic reality for Israel and for mankind. This final messianic hope is still ahead of us, still ahead of Israel too, as it struggles with entirely new, unredeemed problems in the Middle East."[6] Jews are far better prepared by their tradition than Christians not to close horizons and stifle self-criticism. But they may be tempted to do so if they feel alone and abandoned in a hostile world, if they are forced to justify their every action to the world.

5. It is these brand new problems facing Israel that are the cause for much of the criticism, also from Christian quarters, leveled against the state—the refugee problem, the annexation of territories, the "aesthetic disfigurement" of the old city by high rises, etc. Some of these criticisms are justified and the problems cry out for solution; many Israelis recognize this better than anyone else. But the fact that the list of reproaches includes criticism of the new apartment buildings on the hills surrounding the old city which, whether they are in keeping with the local scenery or not, are providing badly needed housing for Israel's growing population—while no voice of protest was heard between 1948 and 1967, when the Jordanians systematically desecrated Jewish graves —is evidence enough that all too many Christians still look for any reason, however paltry, to point an accusing finger at Israel.

We are caught in a curious bind, the basis of which I believe is theological, and hence particularly dangerous.

We have inherited, through our common Scriptures, the sense that Israel is a people apart, different from the nations of the earth. For 1,900 years we tended to interpret this difference negatively: the Jews were worse, more evil, than other peoples. Today we go to the opposite extreme (it is even possible, *mirabile dictu,* for the two extremes to co-exist): the Jews are still different; they are, after all, the chosen people; therefore they must be better than other peoples. This sounds edifying. After all, Jewish tradition itself stresses chosenness, difference and a concomitant higher obligation to morality and justice, for the sake of its mission. But when stressed by Christians this difference, this demand to be better than the rest of the world, can become dangerous. It may take only a flip of the coin for this "chosenness" to be lost, denied once more, if Jews do not live up to their high calling.

It is because Jews sense this danger and ambiguity that some of them today want to be done with the concept of chosenness once and for all. That, in a way, is their theological problem. But our problem is to recognize the impurity in our thinking, which can—though it need not—conceal anti-Semitism. Let us squarely face the fact that we apply a double standard to Israel: we expect it to keep its hands clean in the dirty game of politics, when no other nation—least of all our own at this moment—has ever managed to do so.

This dirty game of politics: Israel is new at it, involved in it for the first time in post-biblical times. Those of us who are sympathetic to Israel hope that the state will avoid some of the pitfalls that have beset Christianity's involvement with power during its history. But if it does not, let us be patient, let us not be quick to condemn. If the high ideal of Zionism is ever to be realized, Israel must first of all be given a chance *to be*. Israel must be allowed to live, to work out its own destiny.

6. Let me suggest one more dimension of the religious significance of Israel today. Israel appears to me as an unprecedented, unqualified affirmation of life, and therefore, at least

by implication for the believer, of him who is "the God of the living." I see only two responses possible on the part of Jews to the Holocaust. One is expressed by Richard Rubenstein who speaks for many Christians as well as Jews when he says that Auschwitz spelled the death of God. But there is another response, and it is being given today by Jews everywhere, above all by Israel: in the face of absurd death, unreasoning life. The state of Israel is the Jewish people's answer to Auschwitz, testifying to the continued viability of the exodus event as the normative experience of Judaism, testifying to God's continuing presence in history, because his people—even after the Holocaust—still survive. After Auschwitz the mere existence of the Jew is an affirmation of life.

Knowing as never before the extremity to which being a Jew can lead, Jews continue to have and raise Jewish children. Emil Fackenheim has articulated this better than anyone else.[7] To raise Jewish children after Auschwitz is to deny Hitler a posthumous victory. It is also, perhaps, a re-enacting of the Aqueda, the binding of Isaac by Abraham. Only the Jew today does not know whether, in the last moment, his son will be spared—indeed, the Holocaust speaks the contrary. Is it going too far, then, to say that his faith—the faith even of the secular Jew, who is willing to defend Israel day and night, to die for it so that the people may live—is as great, or greater even, than the faith of him who is the father of our faith? Such a faith can, I believe, spring only out of the ancient exodus experience. Israel is the living witness that this experience of life and salvation is still the deepest resource of Jewish existence.

1. Abraham Heschel. *Israel, An Echo of Eternity*. New York: Farrar, Straus and Giroux, 1967.

2. Jules Isaac. *The Teaching of Contempt. Christian Roots of Anti-Semitism*. New York: Holt, Rinehart and Winston, 1964. Original French edition 1962.

3. Heschel, *op cit*.

4. Irving Greenberg, lecture given at a symposium at Seton Hall University, October 1970; unpublished manuscript.

5. Heschel, *op. cit.*

6. Rosemary Radford Ruether, *Faith and Fratricide*. To be published by Simon and Schuster in 1974.

7. Emil Fackenheim, "Jewish Faith and the Holocaust: A Fragment," *Commentary*. Vol. 64, No. 2 (August 1968).

Why We Still Can't Talk

Monica K. Hellwig

Anyone who has engaged in the Jewish-Christian dialogue with any seriousness and perseverance will be aware that it has not made any substantial progress in the last ten years. This is not to say that the effort has been wasted. There has been considerable consolidation of past achievements, at least on the Christian side. That is to say, many more people have been drawn toward the level of understanding previously achieved by a few highly specialized people. Some of the crudest types of theological anti-Semitism have gradually been expunged from textbooks at all levels. Some minimal effort at mutual understanding between Christians and Jews has become a regular and official feature, at least in most Roman Catholic dioceses, in the form of joint meetings and prayer services, pulpit exchanges, and so

forth.

All this is not to be despised. It is solid progress from the point of view of human decency, and also in terms of what we as Christians say is our basic concern in the world. But those of us who have been involved over the years in the theology of Jewish-Christian relations are aware that immediately beyond such a fairly superficial "good neighbor" program, we run into apparently unmovable obstacles to any further progress in dialogue. This may come as a surprise to those who have not been personally involved in the effort. Moreover, it is quite difficult to explain the reasons for the impasse.

From the Jewish side the problem is often expressed as non-acceptance by Christians of the religious seriousness of Israel. This has many ramifications and is being discussed elsewhere in this issue by Eva Fleischner. In

Monica Hellwig, a noted theologian and author, teaches theology at Georgetown University.

any case, acceptance or non-acceptance of the religious meaning of the state of Israel, crucial as it may be today when that state is being threatened with annihilation, is symptomatic of a more fundamental understanding of what is properly considered religion, what is salvation and what is the relation of man's freedom in the world to the transcendent God. In other words, the state of Israel is for Christians a challenge to their whole understanding of why it is that they are Christians.

It might also be said that from the Jewish side the problem of serious dialogue with Christians focuses around the divinity claim for Jesus. From a Jewish perspective, the attitude of most Christians toward Jesus is simply idolatrous, and idolatry can have no claim to truth. The claim that Jesus is the Christ, or Messiah, might be discussed. Indeed, for some Jews, Jesus may yet turn out to be the Christ, if his followers really bring about the fulfillment of the messianic hopes and the reign of God among men. But the claim of the divinity of Jesus simply can not even be discussed, and because this claim stands at the center of Christian faith, dialogue with Christians is necessarily marginal. The problem is not only that Christians call Jesus the Son of God in a highly specialized sense, quite different from that which might be used of any prophet in Israel, but that this supposes an understanding of God that seems to be quite other than the God that Israel worships.

From the Christian side the obstacles are more subtle but no less real and forbidding. Christians claim that Jesus, who is the Christ, is the one mediator between man and God, so that there is no salvation that is not explicitly or implicitly through faith in Jesus Christ, or more correctly through incorporation in Jesus the Christ, the new Adam who restores the unity of mankind. This assumption does not make it impossible to dialogue with Jews, but it supposes that such a dialogue is carried on between those who understand correctly the design or self-revelation of God in history and those who understand only in part the goal of their striving, or perhaps even misunderstand it. In fact, Christians also claim that only Jesus and his followers grasped and responded to the true vocation of Israel in the decisive moment, and that therefore only Jesus and his followers can since that moment be called the true Israel, other Jews being in schism from the truth and reality of Israel until they accept Jesus as the Christ and only mediator.

The difficulty about these assumptions is that they do not allow for conversation between equal parties, each with its characteristic experience and truth to contribute toward a new and greater understanding for all. They rather set the stage for the conversation in such a way that the inner coherence of the testimony which Christians have to offer in dialogue depends on a fundamental rejection of Judaism and its experience since Jesus. The conversation really begins with the Christian assuming he knows more about the real meaning of Judaism than the Jew does, and giving Judaism only a conditional value because it may yet lead to an acceptance of Jesus as the Christ.

Under these circumstances it is extremely difficult for us who are Christians even to hear what the Jews are saying about themselves and about us and about mankind before God. It is probably much easier for us to hear what Hindus and Buddhists are saying, because our own self-definition as a religious community does not depend on it. Nevertheless, it would seem that the time is ripe for a new breakthrough, because Christian theology has undergone a rather radical growth from within. We have had to re-examine the conceptual framwork in which we have tried to formulate our experience of salvation in Jesus the Christ, because the questions we have been asking in our times could not be answered in that framework. We have had to re-examine some of our religious language that assumed an understanding of the inner reality of God and made him a bodyless, timeless super-mind, a philosophical construct, necessary to give an ultimate basis to causality and harmony in the natural universe including man. We have had to rediscover that our God is only known and defined in terms of the experience of the believing community that has recognized wonderful works of mercy and compassion in the history of men. Our language has had to become somewhat humbler and more cautious concerning what we know of the mystery of God.

At the same time, we have had to re-examine our religious language concerning revelation, because of the impact of modern Scripture scholarship and of historical studies in the development of doctrine. Once we can trace how different statements of Christian faith came to be, we have to admit that the declarations of faith that we have in the various creeds and church confessions and standard expositions were not received in language from a heavenly source. Rather they are the outcome of long and painstaking efforts within the community of believers to give an account of their experience of God's mercy and salvation in words that would make sense to other men. Words were usually chosen because they already had a meaning that was similar or analogous and could be expanded. These words expressed the experience of believers in terms of the understanding they then had of science, psychology, political and economic structure, the customs of other peoples, and the history and geography of their world. Once we have realized this, we know that the words of our creeds and other statements of faith are not divinely chosen, or the only ones that fit, or even the best ones. In other words, we know that the existing formulations are not sacrosanct, or untouchable, though obviously they command respect because of their origin and the role they have already played in supporting the unity of the churches in understanding and effort.

There is another area within which we have had rapid and radical growth in our times. It is the understanding of the human, of what it means to be human, of what fulfillment is in a human existence, of what the freedom of a human person is and what may be the freedom of a whole society to create its future in the world. We have realized that our values and perceptions and decisions are formed in great dependence on one another and that the responsibility of the individual person may be more limited in one sense than a traditional Western philosophy of man assumed. At the same time we have realized that much that was formerly considered "nature" or "God-given" in the public structure of human societies (the differences between rich and poor, the patterns of exploitation of the weak, the constant recurrence of wars) is man-made and under the control of men if they will acknowledge and fulfill their public responsibilities. Much in our modern experience and our modern scholarship has given new insights into the ways in which individual men and whole societies of men are "man-made." In the light of this, our understanding of the relation of man's freedom to God, of the nature of redemption and of the mode of revelation has simply had to grow.

In that context there emerge some new possibilities for a theological model for Jewish-Christian relations from the Christian side. In the first place, simply looking at the historical development of Christianity out of Judaism, we see that our experience of the salvation of God offered us in Jesus as the Christ can not be ex-plained at all except in terms of Israel's previous expectation of the fulfillment of God's promises to establish his reign of peace, justice, well-being and universal brotherhood among men. There is no way that Christians can dialogue with Jews a-historically. There is no way they can tell the beginning of their own story, because the Christian story begins with a reinterpretation, on the basis of the early community's personal experience, of the religious heritage of Israel as the early Christians had learned it as Jews. Therefore, the first rudimentary framework for a theological model of Christian-Jewish relations really has to be the assumption that the dialogue is structured by the Jewish frame of reference rather than the Christian. That means that we who are Christians must learn to think of our identity as that of a sect of Jews who have acquired a huge Gentile membership. We claim a prophetic calling and role within Israel and consider ourselves bound both to listen to the *continuing* experience of the People (within which we are still in one sense a minority) and to testify within the People to our own experience of Jesus as Christ. We must try to explain to Jewish friends, in terms of their *present* understanding of the promises of God and the meaning of Israel's history, just exactly why, for us, Jesus in his death and in our experience of his resurrection makes the breakthrough that anticipates the reign of God and the fulfillment of all that men have learned to dare to hope for.

Once we do this, we find that the theological model for Christian-Jewish relations also acquires a different perspective in time and history. We find that our claim to be the "true" Israel is not a statement about the past and about what has in fact been accomplished, but rather a prophetic declaration about the future, expressing a confident hope about something that has never yet happened. We base this hope on an experience in which we, but not others, have shared and which allowed us to glimpse a possibility with such dazzling clarity that we are willing to stake everything and commit all our resources to its realization.

In other words, such a theological model really demands the posture that Jesus is for us and in our experience the Christ. For us and in our experience, he is the key and even the horizon of intelligibility for all human existence and all human history, because he is the key and even the horizon for all that man can hope and has not yet learned to hope. But this experience is not accessible to others unless we make it accessible, and because we constantly fail to realize the dream it may never become accessible to all. There is a sense in which Jesus is not yet the Christ for those outside the Christian community and perhaps for many who are institutionally within the community. We who are Christians are making a total claim, but we are making it only on our own experience.

We are making a total claim on the basis only of our own experience and we are still trying to understand that experience, to interpret it in a way of life and to interpret it in words of explanation. We learn that our way of life and our explanations are not an adequate interpretation when we utter them to sincere persons in the community and tradition of Israel and the utterance makes no sense to them. We have to take their response seriously because what we are trying to interpret is precisely the experience that we claim is the self-validating fulfillment of Israel's hope. We have to take it seriously not only in the sense of strategic changes in approach and vocabulary and mode of presentation, but also in the sense of questioning the very substance as we understood it.

Perhaps what is most crucial in a theological model for Christian-Jewish relations is that we acknowledge the total mysteriousness of the claim that it is Jesus who is to "come again" in glory and fulfillment. Not the truth of this claim, but what it might mean ought to be matter for further reflection in dialogue. We need to acknowledge that we have not the faintest idea what it may mean concretely that when the fulfillment of the promises of God comes in the realization of his reign among all men, we Christians expect to be able to recognize Jesus as the heart or core of that realization. We have everything to learn by listening to what the Jews of our time expect of that same fulfillment.

Similarly, the dialogue with Israel can only begin in earnest when we acknowledge the utter mysteriousness of our assertion that Jesus is the Son of God uniquely and in terms of his very being. It is not the truth of the divinity claim but the content of it that demands further careful reflection, and nothing could be more pertinent to that reflection than the Jewish understanding both of God and of man in every era of Jewish history, from the most primitive era even to the present.

In other words, the dialogue can begin seriously when we acknowledge that we are both in pursuit of the reign of God, that we Christians draw our understanding of God and of his promised reign among men from the Jewish tradition, that we experienced an awakening to that reign in the person of Jesus when we saw him as the promised Messiah, and that our theologizing ever since has been intended as an effort to clarify the meaning of that experience in terms of the languages, cultures, philosophies and religious expectations of the people who joined our quest. Human language never yields ultimate reality. We do the best we can with it, and after that we frequently have to ask whether we can do better.

THE JEWISHNESS OF JESUS

Thomas Suriano

Thomas Suriano, a Catholic priest of Diocese of Milwaukee, teaches at St. Francis School of Pastoral Ministry. He received his licentiate of Sacred Theology at The Catholic University and a licentiate of Sacred Scripture from the Biblical Institute.

Scholars, students, preachers, and workaday Christians—we are all asking ourselves anew: How might we come to understand Jesus and his work? Or more succinctly still: What was Jesus like?

In this matter we have some questions again, where even a few years ago we felt we had answers. Paradoxically, modern Scripture research has done us this "service": it has taught us anew some of the things which we do *not* know about Jesus.

At root, of course, is the way we read the Gospels. Modern Gospel research has helped us to see how theological imagery and even poetry-like allusions fill the narratives about Jesus. Numerous details which we once understood literally, almost photographically, are now recognized as symbols conveying a theological (not a biographical) fact about Jesus. Dare we say it thus: We are discovering more accurately how the evangelists wrote.

Those who follow Gospel research carefully (or those who listen to sermons carefully) note one effect of this upon our understanding of Jesus: in a backhanded way scholars are inserting Jesus back into his day. Our misunderstandings of Jesus' life tended to make him not one of us after all. His vision of life, his discourse, his daily dealings were seen as so extraordinary on an observable level that we were genuinely hard-pressed to see how Jesus really was human. So unlike-any-other had Jesus become in our minds that he surely could not be understood as a Jew within the Judaism of his day. (For some it even became difficult to imagine him as a man amid the mankind of his day.)

On the contrary, Jesus was a Jew of his day. He was a man of his day. Vigorously so, I suspect. Hence to understand Jesus, we must understand some of the color, mentality, and thought of Palestinian Judaism in his time.

In one sense the task is bigger than all of us. Volumes could be written on the subject, and indeed are being written. It suffices for our purposes to mention at least a few of the chords which contributed to the symphony which was the Judaism of Jesus' day. We shall remind ourselves of three subjects in particular: the Bible and especially the Torah; the temple; the Pharisees. Obviously we cannot be exhaustive regarding these themes. We shall only offer a few considerations, and then we shall attempt to draw a focus upon Jesus.

Specifically we shall try to surmise how Jesus might have acted and/or understood himself in relation to each of these values.

Admittedly, our choice of themes—Bible, especially the Torah, temple, Pharisees—is somewhat arbitrary. Certain other categories might as easily have been chosen. Quite candidly, these categories have been selected because they are among the areas where we Christians tend to misunderstand Jesus-the-Jew most frequently.

We can begin by reminding ourselves of the Hebrew Bible. (By decision we shall use the term "Hebrew Bible" instead of the term "Old Testament." This latter term causes discomfort to some Jews, for whom there is only one Testament, one timeless Testament. In any case, there surely was only one "Testament" in Jesus' time, the Hebrew Bible.) And how the Hebrew Bible has had authority over the Jewish people! In any era, surely in the era of Jesus, and most especially for the Jews in Israel proper, God's Word was seen as the ultimate measure of understanding and of knowledge. It was always present, always valid. It molded personalities. People learned to read and write from the sacred text, and they learned to live! For every day and every problem the Word of God had something compelling to say. Life was subordinated to it, measured and judged by it, defined in relation to it.

Most especially this was true of the Torah or sacred law book of Israel. It was Israel's guide to life. (Even the word "Torah" derives from the Hebrew word "yarah" which means "to rule" or "to guide.")

The Torah is often misunderstood by Christians. Occasionally we suspect that the Torah was only marginally important to Jewish life at the time of Jesus—a substantial error on our part. More often we subconsciously conclude that the Torah must have been a burden, a heavy damper, a common source of frustration, an anchor upon the native joys of life. Wrong again!

Rabbinic theology and even rabbinic stories show the naiveté of such a view. For instance, some "outsiders" are "horrified" to learn the allegedly excessive number of injunctions in Torah: 613 to be exact (365 negative commands and 248 positive commands). But then we learn from the rabbis their conviction that the accomplishment of any one command in a perfect manner secures salvation. Viewed thus, God is not being oppressive, but rather beneficent, in "multiplying" commands. Thereby he is multiplying the likelihood that something will be commanded which the struggling individual can accomplish with total purity of heart.

Again: so high a regard did Jews have for the Mosaic Torah that any person—man, woman, or little child —who uncovered a new insight into the Torah was to be treated with the same respect which was due to Moses himself. Again: the Jew was to have the same fondness for the Torah which a young man feels for his new bride. Again: Solomon Schechter, a celebrated Jewish scholar of this century, used to tell the story of an elderly professor of his who was wont to pace the floor, even before sunrise, on high Jewish holy days, restlessly waiting for sunrise, *so that he could begin to observe the law* for that feast. Again, and perhaps most colorfully of all: one rabbinic tradition said that even God in heaven spends some time every day engaged in the study of the Torah! Such a Torah is surely not a curse; rather it is a joy supreme!

Jesus too was a "son of the book" and a "son of the law." Like every other Jew, Jesus learned to read and write—and live—from the sacred text. Like every other Jew, Jesus developed his understanding of the Father therein! Jesus respected the Torah, loved it, observed it, and indeed must have delighted in it.

At times tensions developed between the spirit and the letter of the Torah, at least as the letter of the Torah was being interpreted in Jesus' day. (Such tensions develop with everybody of religious law, for law cannot spell itself out to include every possibility within the complexity of human life.) And if, in such moments, Christ opted for the spirit of the Torah, this was not to set aside the Torah. Rather it was to stay faithful to the Torah; it was to do what the Torah itself presumed and desired.

Even when Christ confronted fellow Jews over matters of law, he did so not to hold the law in disregard. Rather it was for the opposite reason —to hold tenaciously to the spirit and wisdom of the Torah when these were being threatened by unhealthy legalism.

And so, for our first proposed conclusion: something in us makes many Christians view Jesus as against the Jewish law; actually he was a son of the law to an edifying degree.

For a different vantage point, we turn our attention now to another cornerstone within Judaism, the temple in Jerusalem.

The temple's physical history is colorful and varied! Constructed by Solomon c. 950 B.C.; destroyed by Babylonian conquerors c. 585 B.C.; constructed again by Jews returning from exile c. 515 B.C.; disassembled and reconstructed by Herod the Great, beginning c. 20 B.C. and continued by various rulers throughout the life of Jesus; destroyed finally by the Roman general Titus in the destruction of Jerusalem in 69-70 A.D.

But we must trace another "history" —the "spiritual" history of the temple, or the history of the "spiritual" temple. Recall, of its nature temple worship required religious hearts if it was to have meaning for God or man. Conversely, where faith was superficial, even "elegant" temple worship was hollow, vacuous, superstitious.

External religion (in this case elegant building and liturgical cult) without interior religion (worshipful and loving hearts): this temptation is present to every religious community, and Judaism succumbed to this temptation. Hence the reserved attitude of the prophets toward the temple, and Isaiah, Jeremiah, and Ezekiel fairly outdo one another in condemning hollow temple worship. Recall, for instance, how Jeremiah (Jer. 7:4) actually mimics the people clinging to the temple for their religious confidence while their hearts are irreligious. Finally, as Jeremiah had threatened (Jer. 7:12-15), the temple was destroyed by the Babylonians, and this was viewed as a divine punishment for such hollow worship.

In the subsequent period of exile, Israel found itself amid a new experience. Quite frankly, the Jews now had to worship God without benefit of the temple, or else worship God not at all. Amid this combination of circumstances—Jeremiah's threat, temple destruction, exile—a new religious awareness was dawning for Israel, namely the awareness that God can be present *wherever* he rules men's hearts, and especially *wherever* he is worshiped. Put succinctly: temple worship and the worship of the heart were meant to go together. But if perchance they did not—and Israel now recognized the distinction—then genuine worship where men loved God was more important than worship within temple courts where hearts were distant from God. After the return from exile and the rebuilding of the temple, the struggle persisted to keep the spirit of worship present in the building of worship. For where genuine worship went on, *there* was the "temple." This tension continued even into Jesus' day. Recall, for instance, the monks of Qumran fleeing the worldly worship of the Jerusalem temple of that day, founding their own community of prayer in the desert at Qumran, and boldly referring to their desert monastery as "the temple."

What of Jesus and the temple? To begin, Luke's infancy narrative holds the temple in high regard. It is there that Zachary learned that he was to be the father of John the Baptist (Lk. 1:13). The infant Jesus was carried to the temple to be presented to God (Lk. 2:22). Joseph and Mary journeyed to the temple every year for Passover, and Jesus, at the age of twelve, stayed behind in the temple,

dialoguing with the sages of Israel (Lk. 2:41-50).

The situation changes, however, so that the Gospels picture a Jesus "apparently" hostile to Jewish temple worship. Jesus "cleansed" the temple in a never-to-be-forgotten narrative (Jn. 2:13-25). He continually challenged the Jewish authorities there (Jn. 7:14ff., for instance). Jesus wept over Jerusalem and its temple (Lk. 19:41-44), and sadly predicted the temple's destruction (Mt. 24:3).

Nevertheless, we must understand this situation precisely. True though these facts may be, Jesus never lost respect for the temple. Quite the contrary; he must have reverenced it in every way. Jesus did not reject the temple or its place in Judaism. *Jesus, too, discovered God the Father there.* When Jesus discerned the lowly straits to which the temple had fallen religiously, he must have wept very genuinely.

Jesus was aware of the "spiritual" history of the temple as discussed above. He knew only too well that Israel's heart was supposed to be where its building was. If indeed he did assume a profit-like criticism of temple activities (or even the "cleansing" itself), this was not in repudiation or rejection of the temple; rather it was precisely because he did treasure the temple and wanted it to be all that it was meant to be.

Jesus did not conduct his vocation and ministry by stepping outside the Judaism of his day, as such total rejection of the temple would imply. And working within Judaism of his day, frankly Jesus did not have the perceivable credentials to stand against the temple and the abode of divine presence in this manner. (Even the monks of Qumran viewed their approach as an interim one and as a way of helping to make the one temple of Jerusalem again what is was meant to be.)

So again, in our discussion of the temple, we see how we might erroneously imagine Jesus as setting himself outside Judaism, when in fact the exact opposite was true.

The narrative of Jesus cleansing the temple is a handy incident for demonstrating one reason why our misunderstandings arise about Jesus. Put succinctly: what Jesus said and did during his lifetime is one thing; what the evangelist tried to communicate when he narrated these same events is sometimes another thing entirely.

Consider the evangelist John. Jesus was much closer to the Judaism of his day (c. 30 A.D.) than John and John's Christian community were to the Judaism of their day (c. 90 A.D.). The reason for this difference is the separation which occurred between Judaism and the early Christians during those all-important years between 30 A.D. and 90 A.D. By 90 A.D. the Church was a much more distinctly evolving reality. Its identity and nature were becoming increasingly clear. Both Jew and Christian recognized as never before that the Christians were opposite to Judaism in some of their religious thought (for

instance, regarding the divinity of Jesus). Christians were no longer able to exist and function *within* Judaism, as they had done at first. Rather they formed a new religious community, apart from Judaism, a "new testament."

One motive which led John to write his Gospel was his desire to encourage Christians to stay faithful to their Christian commitment even in 90 A.D. when the separation from Judaism was causing numerous misgivings in their hearts. To indicate, encourage, or "legitimate" this separatist stand of John's Church, the narrative of Jesus cleansing the temple was very handy, even though this was not Jesus' motive for cleansing the temple. In other words, when Jesus cleansed the temple, he was working "within" Judaism. On the other hand, when John wrote, granted the change in circumstances between 30 A.D. and 90 A.D., he was working "outside" Judaism, and he was using this gesture of Jesus to encourage the Christians about the correctness of this position.

This sort of "double meaning" is very common in the Gospels—Jesus having had one motive for some conduct or gesture, and the evangelist communicating some other meaning when he narrated the same incident. It is understandable how the novice reader might miss the subtleties of such a process, but the effect is as we have stated: we end up with some terrible misunderstandings about Jesus. Very often the misunderstandings set Jesus against Judaism in a way which was not real.

We will dip back into Jewish history yet one more time; we shall discuss—for lack of a better term—the "lay movement" in Judaism, and especially the rabbis and the Pharisees.

Recall again the painful and humiliating Babylonian exile. During this time there emerged in nascent form a group of men who took upon themselves the role of teachers within Judaism and preservers of the sacred tradition. What humble beginnings for a crucially important group of individuals, who eventually would be called "rabbis!" Remember: the task of these men arose from utter necessity; the men who assumed this responsibility were laymen; no one decided to found a new office or position for them; their "position" evolved only because these men cared enough to struggle for Judaism's existence during exile.

With the return from exile, the task of these men became increasingly sophisticated, increasingly a part of Jewish life. The rabbis served as *judges,* rendering decisions regarding the Torah; they were *trustees of a tradition,* stewards of Jewish thought, belief, and behavior; finally—and most importantly—they were *scholar-teachers,* instructing the community, and surrounding themselves with students who would carry on their work as their successors.

Paradoxical as it may seem, the rabbis became the storm-center of severe controversy previous to the time of Jesus. The issue of debate was this: the legitimacy of their authority; for the rabbis had unwittingly moved in upon the priestly caste's sphere of moral influence in Judaism. Remember, the rabbis were carrying out a "non-biblical" office; they did not have the credentials from the Torah. Moreover, the rabbis consulted and used the emerging oral traditions within Judaism; this too was most offensive to most priests, who preferred only the written word of the Torah itself, however mute the Torah may have been regarding certain complexities of ever-evolving society. Then, of course, the rabbis were "laymen" whose influence over the people stung the pride of priests who were less influential, often because they had fallen upon worldly ways.

In effect many Jews turned to the rabbi in a synagogue to discover their God. The Bible was no longer the cultic possession of the priests alone. The synagogue with its instruction and prayer took its place alongside the temple, seat of official sacrifice.

We should recall the Pharisees in this context, for they too found themselves in a similar predicament. They too were considered holy men among Jews. The very word "Pharisee" means "separated" or "set aside." And these individuals fervently "set themselves" aside from defiling contact with any Greeks or Romans in their midst, and from Greek or Roman cultural influences in their midst. With equal rigor the Pharisees "separated themselves" from those within Judaism, fellow Jews, who were less devout than they. Meanwhile they themselves pursued holiness with a passion.

Little wonder that the man-on-the-street Jews held the Pharisees in such high regard. Little wonder that the Pharisees became so influential in Jewish society, especially among the masses who were prevented by poverty from studying the Torah or from having time to abide by the Torah's subtleties. What the common man secretly longed to be in relation to the Torah, the Pharisee had in fact become, and he won the proportionate respect.

And thus it was that the Pharisees too incurred the wrath of jealous worldly priests at the time of Jesus, even as the rabbis had done. Many rabbis may have been Pharisees. In any case, the Pharisees were yet another group of laymen outshining the priests.

It is a caricature to imagine that all or even most of the Pharisees were unworthy of the high respect accorded them. This is a common misunderstanding in Christian minds because of the Gospel condemnation of the Pharisees. We must remember though that the Gospels speak only of a minority of Pharisees. The Pharisees, like every religious school of thought, did have their "fringe group," their minority of men learned in the letter of the law but distant from its vivifying spirit. This minority of Pharisees deserved every condemnation which it received from Jesus. But it was a minority within Pharisaism, distant not only from the spirit of the law, but distant as well

from the spirit of the vast majority of Pharisees. Precisely because of their "irreligious" attitude, these were the Pharisees whom Jesus confronted, and hence these were the Pharisees mentioned in the Gospels; and hence our Christian misunderstanding arises. Most of the Pharisees go undiscussed in the Gospels. This fact is in itself something of a backward tribute to the Pharisees, the silence saying that their goodness was so normal and typical of them as hardly to be worthy of note.

Contrary to standing against the rabbis of his day, it seems that his contemporaries actually group Jesus with the rabbis. The Lord's situation was indeed similar to theirs. He too was a layman, he too was learned in the law, he too was a figure of poignant religious influence. He too had no official role within the temple, and probably he came to know God most of all in the synagogue of Nazareth. Indeed Jesus' followers are even described as calling him "rabbi" on more than one occasion (Mark 9:5, 10:51, etc.).

Even conceding the rabbi-like nature of Jesus' work, something in us insists on placing Jesus in rejection of all or most Pharisees. This is probably to err. In much of his religious concern Jesus shared the viewpoints of virtuous Pharisees. He, like them, was working for the continual purification of Judaism. He, like them, respected the oral traditions surrounding the Torah. He, like them, believed in immortality and resurrection, which the Saducean priests rejected bitterly.

Even regarding a working attitude toward the Romans, Jesus perhaps thought more like a Pharisee than like numerous other groups of that day. The Zealots, for instance, had adopted a harshly violent attitude toward the Romans. They viewed it as praiseworthy to murder a Roman if possible, and they sometimes did so. This approach was surely distant from the Jesus of the Sermon on the Mount. The Qumran monks had still another approach; avoiding Roman defilement was another of their several motives for fleeing to the desert. Again, this posture is distant from Christ's, who busied himself with daily life, even street life, in his generation.

While wanting to avoid over-statement here, and while admitting that Jesus stood roundly against the legalist fringe within Judaism, Jesus may actually have had some connections with the Pharisees. He must have had great respect for the "healthier" Pharisees, and conversely they may have held Jesus in high regard—and one or some may even have become his followers.

So again we draw some hopefully clarifying conclusions: contrary to standing against the rabbis of his day, Jesus may indeed have been one of them—not a "Christian rabbi," remember, but a Jewish rabbi among Jews. Likewise, contrary to standing against all of the Pharisees of his day, Jesus probably found fault only with a minority of Pharisees. He probably held the vast majority of Pharisees in high respect, and he very well may have been associated with them in more ways than we have imagined.

Jesus was therefore very much a man of his age. He was this and much more, of course, but he was a man of his day. Amid Judaism he found his identity; amid Judaism he found his God. And it was among Jews that his first followers found Jesus. We Christians readily remember how Jesus was "unlike any other." We tend to overlook another historical, theological, and even psychological fact—namely that in numerous other days Christ's first followers were able to show interest in him precisely because he was so like them!

EDUCATING FOR JEWISH VALUES

Simon Greenberg

"Moral and character education being the goal of life, the duty to train his child was to the Pharisee no less important than that to discipline himself."[1]

Dr. Simon Greenberg, noted scholar and author, has been with The Jewish Theological Seminary of America as Provost and currently as Vice Chancellor since 1946.

Note that Dr. Finkelstein in defining the Pharisaic "goal of life" does not refer to "religious value education" but "moral and character education." My guess would be that to him the two are synonymous. But they are not so to the secular educator, and I presume that the editor suggested "religious value education" as the subject for discussion because he differentiates between the two. "Moral and character education," it is maintained, may be carried on without any reference to "religious values."

There was a time when there was a fairly clear division of labor in the overall area of "moral and character" as well as "religious value" education. The secular moralist was to specify what were the "moral" values to be taught; the theologian, what were the religious values. The problem of the educator was to decide whether these were teachable, and if so how. Who today is bold enough to undertake to identify the "moral" or the "religious" values that are to be taught? If "the sexual relation transcends every conceivable barrier between people, so that race, class religion and gender are of little moment if two people want each other,"[2] and if the impulse to murder must not be resisted because "to refuse to murder is to risk cancer,"[3] and if, to advance the cause of the revolution, truth, loyalty, filial devotion and human life itself are of little moment, then what do we have in mind when we talk of moral or religious education?

Moreover religious leaders in their understandable anxiety to be modern and "relevant" have graciously declared the secularist's moral values as being, in reality, religious values. Hence we should really speak only of "value education." Modern "liberal" religious educators, therefore, find themselves at a loss on how to in-troduce the religious element into their moral instruction. These various aspects of the subject obviously can not be dealt with in a magazine article. But unless one indicates, however briefly, his basic position on what he considers the values to be and what it is that makes them Jewish and religious, whatever he has to say about the manner of educating for those values will be suspended in mid-air, unrelated to identifiable objects and goals.

We shall therefore formulate a number of apodictic statements indicating what we consider to be the Jewish religious values, and why we designate them as Jewish and religious.

We shall then indicate briefly how the Jewish people educated for them in the past and what Jewish educators today are attempting to do about them.

Some Apodictic Statements[4]
A value is a concept which categorizes the intention which motivates an act. An act may be motivated by the intention to be honest, kind, just, self-sacrificing, loyal etc. The values then are honesty, kindness, justice, loyalty, etc. Values as such are neither secular nor religious. However the intention to implement a value requires a rationale. Reason demands an answer to the question why one should exert the necessary extra effort and make the sacrifice which the implementation of values requires of the agent. It is the *rationale which*

is religious or secular, not the act or the value. *A secular rationale* is one which is formulated in terms, every one of which is accessible to the senses. A religious rationale is one which is rationalized in terms *not all of which* are accessible to the senses.[5]

Thus a merchant who intends to give honest value because he hopes thereby to keep his customer is motivated by a secular value. Honesty in business dealings is a religious value only for one who rationalizes it in terms that reach out beyond the sensibly accessible. It is a Jewish value because it is clearly formulated in a text that is authoritative for the adherents of the Jewish religion.[6] The religious values of Judaism, including duties toward God and through him toward ourselves and our fellow man, are most succinctly formulated in the ten commandments and in the 19th chapter of the book of Leviticus.

Though Scripture promises very tangible mundane rewards for the implementation of its values, the rewards are not presented as the rationale of the values. A man may not be interested in the reward. He may not want to be rich or to have his life in this world extended. He may prefer excitement, self-indulgence and transient glory.

One's *dis*interest in the reward may be an adequate rationalization *for him* for his rejection of the value. But one's interest in the reward does not, from the point of view of Scripture, associate the act with a religious value. The act is associated with a religious value only if the agent performing the act intends thereby to fulfill God's will. He may believe that he will be rewarded, but the reward does not inhere in and follow inevitably from the act as the secularist would have it. The reward depends upon God's will. Values are religious only if they are rooted in a transcendental rationale, and only he is a religious personality whose acceptance of these values is associated with some such rationale.

The oft repeated statement that in Judaism there is no bifurcation between the secular and the religious does not mean that the rabbis were not aware of the many attempts to formulate secular rationalizations for what they considered religious values. It means rather that they consciously or subconsciously rejected those rationalizations as being inadequate. They believed that values could be cogently rationalized only religiously. And since they believed that all acts of the human being should be consciously related to a value, they rationalized *all their acts religiously,* so that the rabbinic admonition that *all* one's acts be performed "for the sake of heaven" was not meant to constitute a humanly unachievable goal. This was the Pharisaic goal of life.[7]

Hence the primary religious value, the one which alone can bestow religious quality upon all other values, is an awareness of the divine. The primary task of all religious value education must be that of awakening, nurturing and sustaining such an awareness in us on all levels of our intellectual development. Such an awareness is awakened, nourished and sustained by (a) habit, (b) knowledge, and (c) intellectual comprehension. Jewish educators—like, I believe, most religious value educators—have over the centuries by and large leaned heavily on the first two methods and employed the third only hesitatingly, even during the periods in Jewish history when leading rabbinic authorities not only sanctioned but encouraged it. But the first two methods were employed with extraordinary effectiveness.

The Role of the Home

The awareness of the divine is first awakened and most fully nourished during the early years of life, *and sustained throughout the whole life,* most effectively by the home. The Jewish home probably has a greater variety of religious ceremonial objects and religiously rooted rituals which are *integrally related to the daily routine of living* than any other home. The choice of the food and the manner in which it may be eaten, the dishes to be used, the manner in which the Sabbath and festival tables are to be set, with their candles, wine and challas (two white breads), the benedictions preceding and following every meal, the mezuzah on the doorpost (Deuteronomy 6:9), the tefilin (Deuteronomy 6:8), the talit, the garment with the fringes (Numbers 15:38) worn all day, or at least during the morning prayers, the kippah, the head cover worn all day, but especially during meals and prayers, the elaborate annual Passover home ceremonials, etc.—all contribute toward

transforming the home into a miniature sanctuary, so that from infancy on one lives in an atmosphere which Dr. Max Kadushin has so felicitously designated as "normal mysticism." Nor is it to be imagined that this implies an ever-present somber, solemn "kill-joy" mood. On the contrary such a home constantly radiates the "simcha shel mitzvah," the joy with which one should serve God (Psalm 100:2). Not to rejoice in life is to deny that that which God created, particularly life itself, is good. (Genesis 1:13).

These habits, pregnant with awareness of the divine and ingrained in youth, are the rock foundation of a religious value education. Their impact upon the innermost recesses of one's being is never completely erased no matter what one does or does not do in later life. Nor has there been found a substitute for them to sustain, even in later life, one's awareness of God and his attachment to the religious values of Judaism, both those concretizing man's relation to God and those affecting his relations to himself and his fellow man.

The Role of Learning[8]

Obviously religiously grounded habits alone cannot serve the needs of a mature mind or a full life. They cannot transmit on the conscious level the concepts they are intended to embody. For that, knowledge of a vast literature containing a vast variety of information concerning the duties one owes to God and, because of him, to himself and his fellow man must be learned and repeatedly re-learned. The rabbis were fully aware of the fact that the mere knowledge of a duty is not in itself sufficient to move us to perform it. They knew that it does, however, stimulate, to however slight a degree, a tendency within us to perform it. Hence lifelong study of the Torah—the literature which contains, expounds, and elaborates on the religious values and the manner of their concretization—is tirelessly extolled by the rabbis and repeatedly pronounced by them to be the greatest of all religious values. "One who studies his portion a hundred times is not to be compared to one who studies it a hundred and one times" (Hagigah 9b). Study of the Torah as a lifelong process, beginning as soon as one learns how to speak and ending, with one's last breath, as it were, as the supreme religious value is one of the unique contributions the Pharisees made to the theory and pedagogy of "moral and character education."

Intellectual Comprehension
What role does and should the rational element play in religious value education? The rational faculty demands sensibly accessible evidence that the implementation of the religious values offers rewards that are superior to those attainable through another system of values. The question of the suffering of the righteous and "happiness" of the wicked is repeatedly raised in Scripture, and not only in the book of Job (Jeremiah 12:1; Psalm 73). And when educators today ask not only how to teach religious values, but whether they are at

all teachable, what I believe they really have in mind is the question of whether there is any cogent way of convincing a person that honesty is to be preferred to dishonesty in circumstances when the tangible, mundane advantages it offers obviously far outdistance those offered by honesty. Is there a cogent secular argument against "swapping wives" or husbands, or even against genocide? These questions face the secular moralist as well as the religious educator, and in attempting to answer them the secularist is, I believe, at a greater disadvantage than the religionist.[9] But this is, or should be, of little comfort to the religionist, because reason can not serve as a substitute for faith, and our problem is to make faith not only reasonable but imperative. And how does one rationalize abstaining from certain forms of work on the Sabbath and holy days, or the observance of dietary laws?

During most eras in Jewish history this problem was simply ignored. The general attitude was that one should not ask for reasons to do what the Lord commands. But in the days of Maimonides they did ask, and in our day they do ask. And even if they would not ask, modern religious educators should not be satisfied with "blind obedience," with ignoring the scientific and historic data at our disposal which were not available to previous generations. That data will be made available to our young people regardless of what we do, and if we do not help them to integrate such data into an overall organically and intellectually acceptable structure, they will either reject their religious values or encapsulate them in a "reason-free" compartment of the mind.

The educators in every branch of the Jewish religious tradition are coping today with this problem, some more and some less vigorously. The Samuel Melton Educational Research Project associated with the Jewish Theological Seminary is today probably making the best directed and best financial effort in this area. Without in any way minimizing the role of habit, of study—good hard study of texts—or of faith, it is attempting to utilize in accordance with the best available pedagogic principles the rational resources of the pupil in order to sustain him in his confrontation with the challenges that modern life presents not only to Jewish religious values but all religions, and even "traditional" secular values.

Not all of the traditional Jewish religious values are with equal vigor urged upon the pupils. For the overwhelming number of modern, secular, well-trained Jews, the selective process is inevitable. That in itself raises highly complex issues. Reason and an historic sense play a greater role in the selective process than in the process of educating for any particular value. That is what makes being a Jewish religious educator today so difficult a task spiritually and intellectually. But that is what also makes it spiritually and intellectually so exciting a task.

1. Louis Finkelstein. *The Pharisees* (Philadelphia: The Jewish Publication Society of America, 3rd revised edition, 1962), p. xxxix.

2. Allen Guttman, *The Jewish Writer in America* (New York: Oxford University Press, 1971), p. 152, where he discusses Paul Goodman's *Making Do* (1963).

3. *Ibid.* p. 167, discussing Norman Mailer's *Advertisement for Myself* in which "Mailer had attempted to clarify his argument about the morality of violence" (p. 166).

4. These statements are fully elaborated in the essay "Ethics, Religion and Judaism by Simon Greenberg in *Conservative Judaism*, published by the Rabbinical Assembly, New York, in Volume XXVI, Number 4, Summer 1972, pp. 85-126 and Volume XXVII, Number 1, Fall 1972, pp. 75-126.

5. *Ibid.*, XXVI, 4, pp. 91-94.

6. Leviticus 1935-36; Deuteronomy 25:13-15.

7. *Conservative Judaism* XXVII, 1, pp. 78-85.

8. For an elaboration of this section see Simon Greenberg "Lifetime Education in the Jewish Tradition," *Religious Education*, May-June 1973.

9. For a critique of secularist ethics, see *Conservative Judaism* XXVI, 4, pp. 94-126.

Jews: Some Christians Are Their Best Friends

Bernhard E. Olson

It would be futile to deny that theological factors do in truth predispose Christians to antipathy toward Jews

Bernhard Olson is the director of Inter-Religious Affairs of the National Conference of Christian Jews.

and Judaism. I explored this relationship at Yale Divinity School in the 1950's. However, while my investigation uncovered a connection between conservative theologies and a negative portrait of Jews, there is no hard evidence that this relationship is integral to the evangelical faith. On the contrary, anti-Judaism contradicts the biblical faith at its core.

The findings of the Yale study were first reported in 1959 in *The Victims and the Oppressors*, a massive but limited paperbound edition distributed to Protestant curriculum editors and human relations agencies, including the Anti-Defamation League of B'nai B'rith. At my request, Dr. Charles Y. Glock made a critique of it. This happenstance made possible the University of California survey, conducted by Glock and Rodney Stark for the ADL, to test the hypothesis that the particularism of salvific and Christological doctrine produced anti-Semitism. Their report, *Christian Beliefs and Anti-Semitism*, was issued in 1966 by Harper and Row, and instantly polarized the Christian community. By extrapolations of its findings, liberal Christians looked down on conservative Christians with fierce superiority. The latter, in turn, fought back defensively.

Jews, by and large, listened to the intra-Christian debate with traumatic results. Their centuries-long suspicions that "essential Christianity" was itself the basic—perhaps even the sole—cause of hatred toward Jews and Judaism seemed to them now to be confirmed by a definitive scientific survey. True, many responsible Jewish leaders steadfastly resisted this conclusion, yet others embraced it.

Thus, the launching of Key '73 automatically aroused in some Jews the conviction that this evangelical effort was *inherently* anti-Semitic and dedicated to the extermination of the Jewish people. Others, more critical of the Glock-Stark findings, were more intent to raise certain legitimate issues that some Key '73 leaders had not adequately assessed—the equation of Christianity with patriotism, the nature of civil religion, and continuity between Judaism and Christianity.

Ironically, the very studies (including my own) intended to raise the level of Christian sensitivity to anti-Semitism aroused in Jews a mounting distrust of the bulk of Christians. One Jewish leader, an intimate friend, confessed that the Glock-Stark findings aroused in him "a deep resentment" against evangelicals and conservative Catholics. But this situation changed radically when the Six-Day War of 1967 burst on the world scene.

Across the land, rabbis turned for support to the Christian clergy, but found that, with some notable exceptions, many theological liberals—especially those who took pride in their "universal commitments"—were unwilling even to support the elemental right of Israel to exist. In contrast, earnest support for Israel poured forth from the conservative, fundamentalist, and evangelical camps. Because of this unanticipated turn of events, Jews and Christians set themselves the fresh task of exploring the theological questions more profoundly.

As the dialogue proceeded, Jews experienced a renewal of their Jewishness through a fresh awareness that the

Jewish religion was integrally tied to people, land, and state by virtue of their covenanted relationship with God. They also increasingly realized, in the words of Rabbi Irving Greenberg, that only those Christians who "took the covenant of God with Abraham seriously" could fully accept the Jews on the basis of their own self-definition. Because of this realization, many Jews thereafter put a large question mark over against the popular indictment of "Christian particularism."

Particularism *per se* Glock and Stark interpret as the refusal to grant "religious legitimacy" to others. Their thesis is that the orthodoxy of a person's convictions (e.g., belief in a personal God and in the divinity of Jesus), plus his particularism (e.g., that belief in Jesus Christ is necessary to salvation), causes religious hostility to Jews which, in turn, produces secular anti-Semitism. The obvious implications of this conclusion are that, in order to destroy anti-Semitism, Christians must either (1) reject the Christian affirmations (thus crushing anti-Semitism at its fount), or (2) "break the casual chain" at a later point by injecting into Christianity antidotes to anti-Semitism derived from outside sources (secular "religious libertarianism," for example).

As an evangelical Christian brought up in the tradition of the Free Churches, where Christian Zionism reigns, whose theology assigns to the Jewish people a central role in history, where "true faith" was inextrica-

bly tied to a free conscience and religious liberty, I already knew inwardly that there already exists in the Christian mainstreams strong currents for precisely such "religious libertarianism" for which Glock and Stark plead. William Penn and Roger Williams needed no recourse outside of their own distinctive Christian understanding of God, man, and society for granting full religious and civil liberty for Jews; the very particularity of their faiths required such universal liberty, without which they could not be Christian at all!

Regrettably, Christians push to the periphery those very factors in Christian teaching that make for a positive Christian embrace of the Jewish people. My own studies demonstrate that idolatrous faiths have invaded Christian theological systems, the churches, and the lives of Christians through accommodations to their host cultures. That is why, as an evangelical, I unequivocally affirm that anti-Semitism in the churches is evidence of heresy and apostasy. Anti-Semitism in any form should alert Christians to the danger of their sub-Christian and anti-Christian commitments. The low priority of anti-Semitism on the Christian agenda is alarming, not only because it threatens Jewish existence, but also and foremost because it threatens authentic Christian existence and witness. The theological exploration of anti-Semitism is therefore an obligatory, rather than an optional, task for the Church, and it must take no less than first place. In this theological reassessment, however, Christians need not turn to centers foreign to their faith, but to their own neglected fount of faith, which has roots in the people Israel.

I

Beyond these introductory remarks, I wish to make three principal points in this essay. The first is that there is a watershed between two kinds of particularism and universalism. One type of particularity-universality is that which centers in one's own *belief-system.* The other type centers in one's own *group.*

Olson's *Faith and Prejudice* (Yale, 1963) contains a chapter to which only Milton Himmelfarb and Franklin H. Littell have paid attention. In it two contrasting faith perspectives are examined. The first set of beliefs are, theologically, universalistic; the second set is, by the same criteria, particularistic. That is to say, the universalistic dogma articulates a global, almost cosmic concern; it deplores any religion that proclaims doctrines of "the chosen people," "revelation," and "uniqueness." It holds that there is not one but "many roads to truth," that there is not one Savior but "many saviors," that no one can lay claim to divine revelation, that to hold a belief that all men cannot accept is divisive, narrow, and bigoted. In contrast, the theologically particularistic dogma affirms that Jesus Christ is Lord and Savior, accepts the idea of chosenness, special revelation, the primacy of "the Word of God" speaking through Scripture, and the uniqueness of the Christian claim.

Yet, strikingly, *both* these universalistic and particularistic views are found in the Yale study to be unprejudiced, anti-ethnocentric, and free of anti-Semitism. How is that possible? Because "both seek to state and implement the anti-ethnocentric genius of their own faith" in the following manner: "Both grant to other groups the same rights which they claim for their own. Both place themselves 'inside' other groups, are able to acknowledge and sympathize with their plights and problems and to understand their views. Their concern for people crosses all group lines unconditionally. There are no obligations imposed on members toward their own group which are not also considered obligations toward members of other groups. All peoples are, essentially, looked at in the same ways from the standpoint of their humanity, dignity, rights, and obligations" (p. 49).

Thus, despite their contrasting theologies, both faiths produce positive portraits of Jews and Judaism because of their ethical universalism. Each faith affirms out of its own perspective the anti-anti-Semitic ways that are indigenous to itself.

The Yale study, however, also identified a religious *ethical particularism* which is anti-Jewish and which centers inwardly on the group. Christian writers who exhibit anti-Semitism appeal to the Church (or the Christian community) as the ultimate source of their values, and as that which they most highly value. When moral obligations are mentioned, it is solely the Christian's ethical obligation to his fellow Christian or "brother-in-the-faith" that is in view. These Christians assume that their own group justly enjoys rights they never urge their fellow Christians to seek for others. They are insensitive to the plight of Jews, and silent on wrongs suffered by outsiders. Their internal histories are idealized in such a way that Christians are never required to face the presence of sin in the Church. Obviously, these writers are guilty of idolatry. They place that ultimate concern and trust in the Church which rightly belongs to God alone.

When to such idolatry of the Church the writer adds other idolatries (such as racism and nationalism), he compounds the felony. Many fundamentalist spokesmen speak much of God, Christ, Savior, salvation, Gospel, and so on, but the verbiage is only surface play for the underlying nationalism and racism to which they are basically committed. Evangelical zeal and the terminology of piety are too often unconscious camouflage for apostasy. And this insight comes most forcefully from perceptive evangelicals themselves.

This type of ethnocentric particularism has great anti-Semitic potential. But it also holds at the heart of Christianity the knife of death.

II

Students of theological anti-Semitism almost totally ignore the anti-Semitic thrust in theological universalism.

Among Christians, nowhere is this thrust more evident than when the subject of the state of Israel is raised.

A vague, free-floating universalism marches under many banners—theistic monism, the religion of humanity, the worship of reason, or the cult of nature. Whatever form it takes, this perennial philosophy is scandalized by anything that does not take on cosmic proportions.

In this universalistic view, the cosmic God of theological universalism is "too big" to be concerned overmuch with "a little piece of real estate" (Israel) in the Middle East, or an obscure people, the Jews. The very establishment of the state of Israel is judged by it to be a reversion to the tribalism and "tribal religion" of the Old Testament. Reliance on the promises of a presumed primitive deity is disclaimed as untenable and parochial in this enlightened age.

A theological liberal, Fred G. Bratton, intends to castigate Christian anti-Semitism in a book called *The Crime of Christendom*, published in 1969 by Beacon Press. But in this work, Bratton also chastizes those Jews who hold that the Jews are a chosen people. He warns: "Ethnic and cultural anti-Semitism . . . was originally provoked and continuously nourished by the orthodox dogmas of uniqueness." Anti-Semitism is justified in Christian minds as a "defense measure" against such claims.

However, the more important issue is "the Jewish dilemma," as Bratton terms it, which consists of the either-or choice he sets before Jews, namely, to become either universalistic or nationalistic. "Many Jews and Christians of the liberal school," he says, "would see the solution of this problem in a cultural assimilation and in recognition that the Jews do not represent a nation or a race but a cultural and religious community."

It is the state of Israel, in Bratton's view, that confronts the Jew with this choice. In the book's closing chapter, Bratton says: "The question facing world Jewry is this: which of the two pictures is primary—assimilation or segregation, religion or nationalism, humanism or tribalism; in short, Judaism or Israel?" Notice how he equates assimilation, humanism, and religion with Judaism, while their opposites, self-segregation, nationalism, and tribalism are equated with Israel!

Bratton's reply to his own question is found in the climactic prose on the last two pages of the book: "The future effectiveness of both Judaism and Christianity ultimately turns on the ontological argument.... Is God a tribal deity or a universal reality? Is he interested in revealing himself only at a certain point in time, at a certain place, through a certain man, to a certain people? Is God concerned only with Hebrew history or Christian history? Is God the God of this planet only, or is he the cosmic consciousness?"

Such views amply demonstrate that the mentality that is scandalized by *Christian* particularism will inevitably be scandalized by *Jewish* particularism. "Only a cosmic universal faith can raise man above the particularisms of the cult," he concludes.

Furthermore, Bratton's religion of "higher immanence," ethical humanism, and "faith that the best is yet to be," on close examination, turns out to be just another competing particularistic faith that says, in effect, to both Jew and Christian, "Your beliefs are wrong, mine are right, and you must remake your faith into one compatible with mine."

Since Bratton's universalism is unitarian, however, some persons may wonder how liberal trinitarian universalism differs from it. For three decades of this century, during the Hitlerian and post-Hitlerian era, *The Christian Century* was the spokesman for Christian liberal universalism. Hertzel Fishman, in a recent book, *American Protestantism and a Jewish State*, documents how the then-editors of the *Century* were throughout this era deeply and repeatedly offended by American Jews on three counts: "They retained a distinctive culture, they felt a common solidarity of peoplehood or race, and their religion was essentially separatist rather than primarily universalist." As the Holocaust began to take its toll, the *Century* opposed attempts by European Jews to emigrate to Palestine, staunchly opposed changing American immigration quotas to permit Jewish refugees to enter, and criticized American Jews who revealed the existence of the death camps.

There exist, then, certain kinds of free-floating Christian theological universalism that have the same potential for anti-Semitism as do certain kinds of theological particularism, despite the former's rejection of racism and nationalism. Moreover, the universalistic accommodation to the third world view of the West, which permits it to see in the small state of Israel a Western imperialistic creation, appeals to the youth of the West. This universalist religion of humanity, under any guise, Christian or secular, is more palatable to the American people than the Nazi philosophy could ever be in its hostility to the Jewish people and the state of Israel.

III

Obviously, the categories of universalism-particularism as a theological model for understanding anti-Semitism are useful, although insufficient. They need not only to be supplemented by additional models, such as those of continuity-discontinuity and inclusion-displacement, (which cannot adequately be treated here), but also clarified.

First, the role of universality and particularity in Christian thought and action needs to be rethought. For example, both universality and particularity are necessary to genuine Christianity, provided that they are of the proper type and mixture.

Particularity is essential because it represents the concrete history of the Christian faith. To ask a Christian to give it up is to ask him to surrender his identity, his reason for being, and to become indistinguishable from the host culture in which he witnesses.

After all, all existence, all life, all history, all experience is concrete and particular. It is here, in this place, now, at this very moment, that I meet God in my neighbor and respond to God's action and call. All events are particular, and in and through them God's action is known. For the Christian as for the Jew, history is the scene of God's action, and must be known in its uniqueness, concreteness, and particularity.

Israel's history and the history of the Church are, therefore, unique. This Decalogue was given at Mount Sinai to this man, Moses. This prophet, Amos, spoke God's Word of judgment in this time and place. It was here, in Egypt, that God through Moses delivered his people from bondage. It is here that Jesus lived, said thus, acted so, died, and was resurrected. In this place the Holy Spirit of God was poured out on all men. Without knowledge of these particular events, we cannot hear God's voice speaking to us, in our concrete situation, in our time. Without particularity, God is mute, unable to reveal himself to those who have ears to hear.

Second, we must appreciate the dialectical *tension* between particularity and universality. Bratton's dilemma is false. The Jew's universality need not wipe out or overpower his particularity, or vice versa. Neither must the Christian allow himself to be pushed into that false either-or.

The harmony of particularism and universalism is made plain by the simplest event. Each event involves both a particular action and circumstance, and yet always asserts something ultimate. If a black man were to move into my block and I were to resent this or try to force him out, particularly I would be rejecting and harassing him. But I would also be asserting, in this particular act, something universal, namely, the implicit right of the white race to determine the fate of blacks. That is to say, I would be acting as though the white race were God. Theologically, I would be committing the idolatry of racism.

So, too, it is with holy history. The act of God freeing Jews from Egyptian slavery—the exodus—is historically particular, but it is also a universal affirmation that God is concerned about injustice everywhere and a mandate to the believer to tackle the serious task of freeing all people from bondage.

Moreover, in this tension between universalism and particularism, there is a mutual corrective. Universalism is centrifugal. It tugs outwardly at us from the center of our individual and group existence. Universalism prevents particularism from turning a group in on itself, and thus becoming the end, or purpose, of its own existence. On the other hand, particularism is centripetal. It keeps us moored to the base of our existence as persons and as groups. It prevents universalism from becoming a mere affirmation of and loyalty to abstractions.

In short, whereas universalism enables the Christian group identifications and witness to escape idolatry, particularism affirms our right to concrete existence, to our uniqueness, to differ from the norm, to resist the pressures of culture to mold us according to its pleasure, and if need be, to witness against the world.

Finally, theological particularism is not necessarily incompatible with ethical universalism. Billy Graham is much nearer the truth when he asserts that the central problem Christians have with Jews is the Christian's mistaken notion that God, in choosing to include the Gentiles in God's promises to Israel, thereby excluded the Jews. Christians did not displace the Jews, says Graham; rather Christians are grafted onto the Jewish people. And that is why Billy Graham, for all his salvific particularity, is a friend of the Jewish people and an enemy of all anti-Semitism.

WHAT CAN A KIBBUTZ TEACH US?

Sr. Miriam Lahey

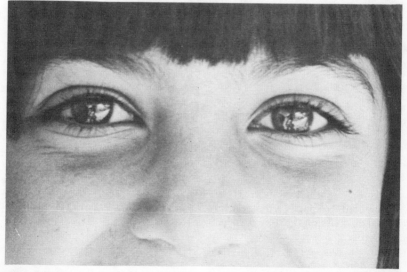

Most kibbutzim include in their membership a group of "volunteers" —persons from outside the country who come to share for a time the kib-

Sister Miriam Lahey, a Carmelite nun, lived for three months in the Haifa Kibbutz. Presently, she is working in a Jewish home for the aged and finishing her doctorate at Catholic University.

butz way of life. At the conclusion of their stay the volunteers are given a certificate: "Presented to_____ as a token of appreciation for having worked and shared with us our kibbutz way of life based on brotherhood and peace—Shalom."

The history of the kubbutz movement

is important in attempting any kind of assessment of the kibbutz as community. In the first place, the kibbutz is something quite unique, a new social experiment with no tradition to follow in its beginning, no model on which to base its efforts.

The founders of the kibbutz movement came from situations where anti-Semitism caused them much suffering and humiliation and greatly limited their freedom. They wanted to be free from oppression, to build a situation where they could live without fear, in brotherhood and peace.

When they came to Israel over fifty years ago, they literally had to carve an existence out of the rock. The society which they sought to build was one based on total sharing, sharing in all the work of living, the work of building a situation in which they could live in security. The original members had to bring forth a life from the rocky soil and their motivation was rooted in a deprived experience against which they were able to measure the value of their communal struggles. By this motivation they were able to respond to the immense demands made on them in the beginning—the hunger, cold, sickness, weariness and other conditions of their pioneer life. Later the memory of this initial struggle served as new motivation for perseverance through the more subtle difficulties of building community. The thought of what they had already invested in terms of physical and psychological labor added value to their kibbutz way of life and strengthened their motivation

to maintain their efforts.

Some years later when Nazism brought new persecution to the European Jewish population, other members came to the kibbutz out of oppression. The arrival of these Jews fleeing from the Holocaust deepened the motivation for perseverance in the kibbutz way of life by their presence as living witness to the need for a place where Jews could live in security and freedom from oppression. Not long after this came the struggle for Israel's independence. For most of the kibbutzniks this meant a renewed zeal for the homeland whose roots were so closely bound up with the roots of their own communal experience. Indeed it was from among the kibbutzim that some of the best functioning military personnel were recruited. Why? Because they had already learned the value of working together toward an ideal, had learned a sense of unified effort. They played an important role in the birth of Israel as a nation, and the emotional energies involved in this achievement brought a deepened sense of pride and loyalty toward the kibbutz which they associated with the birth of Israel.

Of late, immigrants to the kibbutz have not come from oppressed situations, except in the case of Russian Jews. Even these represent immigration on an individual rather than collective basis as evidenced by some of the difficulties they have had with assimilation. While they are warmly received when they come to the kibbutzim, there does not seem to be the same sense of collective motivation associated with their coming or with their reception, as was the case with previous groups.

This brief glance at kibbutz history, especially as affecting motivation, can be of important significance for an examination of other attempts to build community. Fluctuations in motivation are going to affect the bond of community. If the answer to the question "Why have we come hither?" is a vivid and vital one, then the community bond will be a vivid and vital one. The present young generation of kibbutzniks have not shared directly in the experiences which motivated their parents. Each year there is a ceremony of initiation in which the graduates of the kibbutz high school are received formally into full kibbutz membership. This takes place shortly before they leave for their obligatory military service. Recently some of these new members were third-generation kibbutzniks. This means that it was their grandparents who pioneered the kibbutz experiment and their parents who brought to birth the state of Israel. While these young persons have been influenced by their forebears, they have not been motivated by the experience of oppression and deprivation. Any oppression they may have experienced will necessarily have come from within the kibbutz. This is not to suggest that the kibbutz operates as an oppressive society, but realistically to acknowledge that it is not possible to achieve balance between group and individual without some

sacrifice on the part of the individual. Some young persons on the kibbutz express resentment on the issues of education and career option, for instance. The founders of the kibbutz came from a society in which Jews were not permitted to own property, and where in an agrarian economy they were only able to strive for real excellence in areas of scholarship and business. When they came to their new home in Israel, the concept of working the land held more than survival benefits for them; it also had the value of status symbol which was very important to them in the light of their history. This fact, combined with the real necessity of hard physical labor, brought about a deemphasis of things academic and a highlighting of agriculture with its attendant manual labor.

Today's kibbutz youth, while respecting the value of agricultural labor, have not the same status-related need to till the soil as their forefathers had. In fact they are keenly aware of the need for progress in technological knowledge in order to have a part in the future. For this reason some young people are dissatisfied with the general high school education provided them in the kibbutz and seek opportunity for additional study outside. So the question arises: Does specialization break down community? At present the kibbutz cannot answer that question because, as data indicate, the desire for specialization is only now beginning to touch a significant proportion of the members. The question of specialization is a crucial one for any community, and certainly the communities of religious are experiencing this issue as a source of conflict. When group members begin to specialize there is a tendency for their behavior to be regarded as different. Then it is not long before *they* are regarded as deviant, and when that happens the bond of community suffers strain.

Possibly this strain can be better understood if the community is differentiated according to community of purpose or community of persons, or, as classical sociology would describe it, primary group and secondary group. Obviously the kibbutz set itself up as a community of purpose. They came together in order to *do* something. In order to achieve their purpose it was necessary to assign roles and function, to interact in a way which would be consistent with their purpose. It was not possible to consider personal preferences to any great extent. In the beginning, in order to survive and to achieve their purpose, the individual's tastes frequently had to be sacrificed. As one of the original kibbutzniks put it: "The work was backbreaking. We did all kinds of hard work. There was nothing to eat and no water either, and we were often sick. Life was very difficult. Sometimes we didn't have the money even for our most essential needs. Our living quarters and even our food were of the poorest quality, and we had trouble aplenty." In such a situation individual differences were submerged in the pressing experience of need which could be met only by intense communal effort.

Since the individuals had chosen to join this particular purpose group they were willing to accept the sacrifices involved, or else, finding them too difficult, to withdraw. The young kibbutzniks, however, did not make the initial choice of belonging, and this is proving to be of prime significance in terms of individual motivation.

As long as community of purpose can maintain the visibility of purpose and the motivation of the individual members toward that purpose, the bond of community can be maintained. When, however, the purpose begins to lose visibility and/or its motivating power, the bond of the group is threatened.

If a group in its origin came together not as community of purpose but as community of persons, the bond is quite other. Not of course that there is total exclusivity between the two goals, but there is a considerably significant difference between them, and when there is confusion about the difference, expectations may be unrealistic and destined to disappointment. A community of persons, of which the classic example is the family, has such goals as mutual support and care, being together, and strengthening of individual goals by mutuality. It is possible for such a community to tolerate much more diversity and specialization; decision-making takes place informally. For the community of purpose, on the contrary, decisions are made in formal assembly. This kind of community, of which the classic example is the corporation, has for its goal the expeditious achievement of the purpose for which it is set up. Diversity and specialization can be tolerated only insofar as they do not impede the purpose of the community.

The kibbutz, being a community of purpose, makes its members quickly capable of group decision-making in the formal assembly. By contrast, the members are not well prepared to handle decision-making at a personal level and are highly sensitive to the pressure of group expectations, especially from their own peers with whom they have spent the entirety of their formative years. They are very anxious to behave as all the others do.

This strength of peer pressure makes it possible for the kibbutz to function with a very low-profile leadership style. A visitor could live in the kibbutz for months without being aware of who the secretaries are. The democracy of the kibbutz administration is near-utopian but possibly can only be maintained because peer pressure handles many of the group problems, especially areas of deviance.

Because it is a community of purpose, the kibbutz is concerned with the problem of maintaining membership. Bruno Bettleheim in his assessment of kibbutz life found a certain programmed loyalty among the members which possibly has its origin in the need to keep the members at home to do the work of the kibbutz. Here there is contrast with the community of persons which does not seek to keep its members at home, but rather to enable them to go out from the group, to experience such a supportive sense of "home" that they can go out and return without threat to the individuals or the group.

In terms of building effective human community, much can be learned from a study of the kibbutz experiment. It provides a unique opportunity to see a community of purpose which seeks to incorporate elements of community of persons. Its success to date might be partly due to careful distinction between these two elements with awareness on the part of the members that the priorities are in favor of community of purpose, for it was as community of purpose that they came together. Failure to make this distinction will lead to confusion of priorities and a seeking of the best of both worlds which ends up in avoiding responsibilities for either. Failure to make this distinction can also lead to a possessive clutching at personnel which refuses to let members go out from the group and which cannot tolerate diversity of function based on personal option. These attitudes belong properly to community of purpose. If that is what a group wants to be, well and good, but then one cannot appeal to primary group motives; one cannot expect a "family" spirit. Group intimacy does not properly belong to secondary groups. The question of privacy within the group is one which is affected by this confusion of priorities. In the kibbutz there is not much opportunity for privacy. A person who has lived outside the kibbutz and has learned to value privacy will know how to find occasions for it even within the kibbutz, but it does not seem to be a high priority item with kibbutzniks. Many visitors find the lack of privacy difficult, especially regarding, in Goffman's terms, the informational and conversational preserves.

Martin Buber has commented that "the kibbutz is an outstanding example of non-failure." How that success will stand the test of time remains to be seen, but certainly it is clear that those who pioneered the kibbutz experiment have bestowed upon it a great sense of awareness of what it was about. Is it because they were persons of scholarship? Whatever the reason, the book of Proverbs advises that the wise man learns from the experience of the other. In this light a study of the kibbutz way of life can be really profitable for all who are interested in building effective human community. As pointed out above, the collective motivation is highly significant because when the drive toward need-fulfillment is complete, the need will be no longer experienced. In the original group members, the memory of the past felt need can serve as motivation, but this may not be sufficient for the later generations who have not experienced the need. Perhaps this accounts for the move away from the kibbutz and toward the moshave which is beginning. The moshave is also a collective life but includes much more margin for individual expression of life and for personal option. Can we learn from this that there is a certain obsolescence built into any institution? Can we realize that a group solution to any social problem will have to allow a certain margin for newness of life? Possibly nothing evidences the success of the kibbutz experiment as surely as the fact that most kibbutzim are grappling with just this problem. Possibly the greatest contribution to building effective human community which has been made by the kibbutz movement lies in its willingness to assess its own development and to continue to move in the direction of its goals in a manner which is consistent with the present in which it lives now. Sadly, we find that events in the Middle East continue to provide intense motivation for collective efforts there. May we profit from this unique example of collaboration under duress, recognizing the value of group motivation toward a way of life together based, as the kibbutz phrases it, on brotherhood and peace. Shalom!

The Bi-Polar Experience

John T. Pawlikowski

What is a Jew? It has been remarked that if three Jews gather to discuss this question four or more answers are likely to emerge. The moral of this tale is that Judaism is a phenomenon that cannot easily be fitted into our accepted categories of race, ethnic group, religion, etc. Perhaps the

John T. Pawlikowski, O.S.M., is a member of the faculty of the Catholic Theological Union in Chicago. He is a member of the National Council of Churches' Faith & Order Commission on Israel, the Commission of Ecumenism for the Archdiocese of Chicago, and the Catholic Bishops' Secretariat on Catholic-Jewish Relations.

best term developed thus far to describe the complex reality that Judaism represents is peoplehood.

In a recent article in the national Jewish journal *Reconstructionist* Rabbi Gerald Lee Zelizer makes the claim that "no other large-scale organized group on the American scene so systematically tempers ethnicity with religion; or deflates religion from the ethereal to the everyday living experience of ethnicity" ("The Uniqueness of Judaism: 1973," Vol. 39, No. 4, May 1973, p. 12). While

Rabbi Zelizer may somewhat exaggerate Judaism's pre-eminence in this regard, the substance of his remarks hit on a point that any Christian interested in dialogue with Jews must clearly understand: Judaism is not simply another religious tradition but a peoplehood that combines religion with ethnicity and culture in a manner somewhat unique within the American social mosaic. Hence Jewish-Christian dialogue will have to assume a character that differs to some degree from inter-Christian ecumenism where the concentration may more exclusively fall on strictly religious and theological issues.

The recently published books reviewed below will introduce the Christian reader to most of the important areas of concern that stir the contemporary Jewish soul. Several will also provide some introduction to the principal topics on the current Jewish-Christian dialogue agenda.

There exists virtual unanimity among Jewish writers of our day that the two chief realities of 20th-century Jewish life have been the Holocaust (i.e., the slaughter of six million Jews in Nazi Germany) and the creation of the modern state of Israel. No one can really enter into the thought patterns and feelings of the Jewish people today without some grasp of the influence of these two events on their fundamental self-understanding. There is literally no way a Christian can truly communicate with a contemporary Jewish person without a good familiarity of their significance for Judaism throughout the world.

Yet until quite recently both issues were generally omitted from the dialogue on the grounds that they were either too political or involved past history which no longer need concern us. As the conflict in Jewish-Christian dialogue following the Six-Day War in 1967 showed us quite clearly, such omission introduces an atmosphere of unreality that, if allowed to persist, will ultimately subvert the dialogue. This is not to say that all Jews agree on the meaning and implications of these two events for their contemporary existence. Nor are Christians being asked to accept uncritically any particular Jewish viewpoint on these issues. The one *sine qua non*, however, is that the Holocaust and the state of Israel be given high priority in the dialogue and that they be fully and frankly discussed.

Several new publications will more than adequately expose non-Jewish readers to the monumental dimensions of the Holocaust and the state of Israel for 20th-century Judaism. The first, entitled *The Holocaust: The Destruction of European Jewry, 1933-1945* by Professor Nora Levin of Gratz College in Philadelphia (New York, Schocken Books paperback, $6.95), is a comprehensive exposition marked by scrupulous scholarship throughout its 784 pages of the Third Reich's program of extermination of the Jews, the victims' difficulty in anticipating their fate, and the progressive implementation of the so-called Final Solution.

Professor Levin utilizes a chronological approach to present her findings in the first part of the book. Her narrative moves from a consideration of Nazi efforts to force emigration coupled with the almost universal refusal of foreign nations including the United States to accept sizable immigration, to a depiction of life in the ghettos, to the cruelty of the pogroms and the years of deportation. The second part of *The Holocaust* describes what occurred with respect to the Jewish community in the years 1933-1945 country by country. Included at great length in the analysis are the military-political context (with some emphasis on intra-Nazi policy disputes) and the European tradition of anti-Semitism, in particular as these affected Germany's relations with the areas it controlled or occupied. Professor Levin sternly rejects the thesis advanced by Dr. Hannah Arendt that Jewish passivity, combined with a kind of metaphysical complicity, made the Nazi task relatively simple to carry out. Two questions stand out for her: resistance and rescue. Contrary to Dr. Arendt she details significant examples of resistance within various European Jewish communities. More would have helped, she frankly admits, even though for the Germans "winning the war was secondary to killing Jews."

On the rescue issue she makes a rather chilling case for British sabotage of efforts along this line as well as the indifference shown by the United States and the Soviet Union. It might be interjected here that another new work by Saul S. Friedman, *No Haven for the Oppressed: United States Policy toward Jewish Refu-*gees, *1938-1945* (Detroit, Wayne State University Press, 1973, $15.95), offers an even more thorough analysis of this country's policy toward Jewish refugees during World War II. While Friedman takes issue with those who claim that anti-Semitism at the highest levels of the State Department was the major block to rescue efforts in behalf of Jews, he unveils the activities of some officials who continually thwarted rescue plans. A disinclination to engage in negotiations with the Nazis and a fear that any ransom would prolong the global conflict are for him the chief causes for the Allies limiting themselves to only token gestures in support of the Jews.

Returning to Professor Levin's work, Christians will also find of interest her treatment of the Vatican's reaction to the Nazi Holocaust. Her general assessment is that in dealing with this tragedy the Vatican was a victim of its own history of anti-Semitism as well as a product of a historical conditioning as strong as that of any other human institution. The Roman Church in her view needed to discover arenas of power in an era of shrinking religious response and had to weigh the political consequences of impulsively acting out of moral fervor. She appraises Pope Pius XII as a man who undoubtedly believed he was being scrupulously neutral in his handling of world-shattering events but who, admittedly, believed that National Socialism was a lesser evil than Communism. In this context how could Jews be viewed other than as unfortunate expendables?

While the final verdict on Pius XII's position on the Holocaust is not yet in, and may in fact prove to be different from Professor Levin's, Catholics cannot just ignore or easily dismiss her evaluation. This has generally been the case up till now when authors such as Gordon Zahn and Guenter Lewy and the play *The Deputy* painfully raised the issue. The almost universal response by Catholics has been to bury rather than to probe. In addition to the importance of studying the Holocaust in order to better understand our partners in the dialogue, Catholics have a vital need to grapple with the significance of this event for their own self-understanding. For as Professor Franklin Littell of Temple University has remarked, in one sense the Holocaust is something that happened to Christians rather than to the Jews. And as the Catholic philosopher Fredrich Heer of the University of Vienna has added in his book *God's First Love,* our failure to confront the Holocaust is symptomatic of how Catholicism has confronted all other evils, especially war and the possibility of a nuclear holocaust.

Another work that will give Christians a feel for the Jewish Holocaust experience is the novel by Arthur A. Cohen called *In the Days of Simon Stern* (New York, Random House, 1973, $8.95). Set in an enclave of poor Jews in New York City, the story recounts the life of a son of immigrants, fantastically rich, eccentrically learned, by turns playboy and penitent, who takes upon himself the destiny of Messiah of his people.

Cohen's novel is one of a string of recent works which probe the meaning of Jewish life after the horror of the Holocaust. In many ways this is becoming the theological issue in contemporary Judaism. But many of the principal contributors to this new search are not employing the usual theological style but relying rather on the medium of literature. A prime example is the renowned survivor of the Holocaust, Elie Wiesel. Such an approach is in fact quite consistent with Jewish tradition which has tended to shy away from pure theology in trying to express its grasp of God and the God-man relationship. The world of Jewish literature is an excellent avenue whereby a Christian can enter the world of Judaism not only in its ethnic and social aspects but with respect to its theological consciousness as well.

On the question of Israel two works deserve the attention of Christians. The first is Christopher Sykes' *Crossroads to Israel: 1917-1948* (Bloomington, Indiana University Press paperback, 1973, $3.50). It is one of the best critical syntheses of the complex and controversial series of events that led up to the creation of the state of Israel by the United Nations in 1948. The author's style is both exciting and clear and he exhibits a splendid sense of the political drama and human meaning attached to the events of these years. While interested Christians would want to read more than a single work on this situation, this book is an excellent introduction to the whole question.

Another approach to the issue of the

state of Israel from a more specifically Christian perspective can be found in the concluding chapter of Frederick M. Schweitzer's *A History of the Jews since the First Century A.D.* (New York, Macmillan, 1971, $7.95 hardcover, $1.95 paperback). Dr. Schweitzer, a Roman Catholic member of the department of history at Manhattan College, offers a short but clear and scholarly defensible exposition of the rebirth of the state of Israel together with some indication of the meaning of this rebirth for the Christian world.

One might add, however, that Dr. Schweitzer's book will prove valuable not only for its chapter on Israel but in its entirety. It is one of the most readable and coherent appraisals of Jewish history ever produced by a Christian historian. Spanning the entire post-biblical period with special emphasis on contemporary implications, the work is an excellent correction to the centuries of Christian scholars' misrepresentation and neglect of Jewish history. This is especially true of the history of Christianity's persecution of the Jews in past centuries, the accounts of which are generally by-passed in Christian teaching materials. Yet most Jews are painfully aware of this history. Hence there cannot be any genuine sharing in the dialogue until the Christian level of consciousness has been raised to the same level in this regard. *A History of the Jews since the First Century A.D.* is well adapted for use in advanced level high school, in college and in adult education programs as a basic textual resource.

The discussion of Christian writings about Jews and Judaism brings us to another important book in the current dialogue library. *Elder and Younger Brothers: The Encounter of Jews and Christians* by the Protestant scholar A. Roy Eckardt. Dr. Eckardt has been a pioneer in the area of Christian-Jewish relations, and this work, written a few years back but just reissued in paperback (New York, Schocken Books, 1973, $3.45), represents his foremost theological statement on the relationship between the two faith communities. *The Elder and Younger Brothers* is one of the most important theological appraisals of the Church's traditional fulfillment theology vis-à-vis Judaism. A total rethinking of this theology which claims that Christianity completed Judaism and assumed into itself whatever was valuable within its parent is an urgent task at the present hour. Eckardt's book offers some important building blocks for establishing a new theological relationship with respect to Judaism. It should be read in conjunction with the writings of such other groundbreaking authors as Monika Hellwig, Rosemary Ruether, James Parkes, John Oesterreicher and Gregory Baum. While it will take considerably more theological soul-searching by Christians before a new full-blown theology of Judaism can be developed within the Church, our task at the moment is humbly to admit that our past fulfillment theology was highly defective and to firmly proclaim the continuing validity of Judaism as a creative, vital, salvific religious expression after the coming of Christ. The principles we develop in this search will also serve the Christian community well in its necessary and potentially enriching dialogue with all other non-Christian religions.

Eckardt's book not only presents a theological challenge to Christians but a moral one as well. The conclusion cannot be escaped, he says, that a Christian insistence upon redemption has occupied a preponderent place in the Church's ideological justification of its own social dominance. If the Jewish hope for a redeemer has been comparatively weak, the corresponding Christian hope has been nothing but an infinite embarrassment to the Church. The Jew, he insists, is obliged to ask a painful question of his Christian brother: "When you set out the cup of common wine in remembrance of the sufferings of Jesus, what possible *specific* meaning or lesson is embodied in this symbolic act? Are you ready to suffer as Jesus did? Tell me, where were you when we Jews were living and dying in Auschwitz? In sum, just who are the witnesses of the redeemer?" Fr. Edward Flannery the noted expert on anti-Semitism and head of the National Bishops' Secretariat for Catholic-Jewish relations has called *The Elder and Younger Brothers* a work of reconciliation, a title it truly deserves.

Two other publications that will be of interest to those exploring Christian-Jewish relations from a theological perspective are *The Shaping of Jewish History: A Radical New Interpretation* by Ellis Rivkin (New York,

Charles Scribner's Sons, paperback, 1973, $2.65) and Richard L. Rubenstein's *My Brother Paul* (New York, Harper & Row, 1972, $5.95). Rivkin's book is a highly provocative, intensely fascinating interpretation of the meaning of Jewish history. Rivkin is no stranger to interreligious dialogue, and though a historian by trade, many of his ideas have important theological overtones, particularly his unity concept. He himself has found certain similarities in thought if not in language between his ideas and those of the late Teilhard de Chardin. Dr. Rivkin is an economic determinist and an optimistic prophet about the potential of capitalism for the redemption of mankind. Many will take serious exception to this fundamental standpoint of his. Yet many of his remarks about the nature of Jewish history open for those of us who have engaged him in dialogue, as I did in a Catholic-Jewish-Southern Baptist trilogue in Nashville last spring, fascinating possibilities for seeing points of convergence between our respective religious traditions. For me *The Shaping of Jewish History* and Rivkin's writings in general represent some of the most exciting and important contributions to the dialogue made by someone from the Jewish side.

Acquaintance with Rivkin is also important for Christians because of his significant contributions on the development of Pharisaism which he terms a truly revolutionary movement in Judaism Pharisaism remains, despite our many advances in Christian-

Jewish relations since Vatican II, one of the principal sources of negative stereotypes of the Jews in Christian preaching and education. *The Shaping of Jewish History* contains an excellent summary chapter on the Pharisaic revolution that will go a long way in breaking down many of the unwarranted Christian impressions of this progressive movement which has influenced profoundly all forms of post-biblical Judaism and had a significant impact on Jesus and the early Church. This will result in the elimination of an important source of anti-Judaism still surviving in Christian education.

Richard Rubenstein's *My Brother Paul* certainly has to rank as one of the most provocative volumes produced in the area of Christian-Jewish relations in recent times, mainly because Rubenstein himself is a highly controversial figure who has been associated with the Christian death of God theologians. The title of this work is especially significant because even those Jewish authors who in the past have been most open to Christianity have looked upon Paul as a corrupting influence who was responsible for the break between Judaism and Christianity. Many of these authors would have sympathy with some of the teachings of Jesus but little time for Paul. Hence Rabbi Rubenstein is going against a pervasive and long-standing Jewish tradition in his positive portrayal of the apostle.

Rubenstein's approach is psychoanalytical throughout. He sees Paul's developing consciousness as a direct result of his personal and psychic dispositions. For him Paul emerges as a revolutionary Jewish mystic whose insights often anticipate the world of 20th-century psychoanalysis. Rubenstein regards Paul's theological vision as having such universal relevance that it ultimately transcends the faith he helped to found. While Rubenstein is hardly the last word on the subject, his attempt to combine psychology, theology and biblical scholarship cannot be ignored in this era when theology generally is in dialogue with the psychological sciences. This approach must have its voice heard in the theological reconstruction of the Jewish-Christian relationship referred to earlier. And *My Brother Paul* at the minimum will at least provoke some interesting questions in this line.

A final work relevant to Christian-Jewish relations brings up to the practical level of social interaction which it might be said is just as vital for the growth of the dialogue as the theological dimension. The book in question deals with the highly sensitive area of intermarriage. Father Ronald Luka, C.M.F., in *When a Christian and a Jew Marry* (New York, Paulist Press, 1973, $1.25), offers some very practical and soundly ecumenical insights into the problems associated with a Christian-Jewish marriage. The Jewish perspective is introduced by Rabbi Bernard M. Zlotowitz who summarizes well the principal objections to intermarriage currently being put forward by the Jewish community where intermarriage has assumed the dimensions of a national controversy. The rabbi outlines in a sensitive fashion the basic fear of the Jewish community that as a minority in a Gentile society intermarriage could eventually lead to the disintegration of the Jewish people. Luka's book ends with an excellent model for a Christian-Jewish wedding ceremony. This work will prove a valuable resource for priests, Catholics contemplating intermarriage, or families who have relatives involved in or planning a Christian-Jewish marriage.

So far this review has highlighted three major areas of contemporary Jewish concern: the Holocaust, the state of Israel and intermarriage. Another one high on the agenda is the plight of the Jews in the Soviet Union. Christians sometimes fail to recognize that almost one-third of the total present-day membership of the Jewish people resides in the Soviet Union. Hence the grave concern about the survival of this community expressed by world Jewry. Whatever truth there might be to the passivity thesis of Hannah Arendt mentioned above in connection with Nora Levin's book, Jews are determined that no one will ever be able to make that charge with regard to the situation of the Soviet Jews. And sensitive Christians have spoken in similar language through the National Interreligious Task Force on Soviet Jewry. These Christians will not stand by idly and permit a cultural genocide of Jews in the Soviet Union that would have the same ultimate effects as the Nazi program. Concern for Christian-Jewish dialogue now demands of

Christians the raising of their voices in protest in favor of those Jews who wish to live as Jews by emigrating to Israel. Good historical background material on this urgent problem can be secured by reading *The Jews in Soviet Russia since 1917,* edited by Lionel Kochan (New York, Oxford University Press, 1972, $12.50). The scholarly essays in this volume by well-known Jewish historians and Sovietologists offer a comprehensive and authoritative account of the historical, sociological and ideological factors underlying the present crucial situation.

This review essay began with the assertion that to understand Judaism one must probe both the Jew's religious heritage and his ethno-cultural heritage. In conclusion, brief reference should be made to three works that will further enlighten a Christian's understanding of the second part of this Jewish bipolarity.

The first work is *The Jews of Modernity* by Milton Himmelfarb (New York, Basic Books, 1973, $10.95). The author is a widely known commentator on Jewish cultural life and on the relationship of religion and culture. His writings frequently appear in the respected Jewish periodical *Commentary* where many of the book's essays were first published. While some Jews look upon Himmelfarb as too conservative and skeptical in his outlook, his viewpoints are always challenging and he has had considerable experience in the dialogue.

The dominant theme of the essays collected in this volume is the tension which exists between tradition and modernity, between particularism and universalism in the Jewish soul and in the Jewish community. Himmelfarb particularly attacks that form of modernity he finds disproportionately favored by Jews which tends toward liberal, messianic politics and which he feels substitutes art and science for genuine religion.

American Judaism: Adventures in Modernity (Englewood Cliffs, N.J., Prentice-Hall, 1973) is another interpretive exposition of how Jews have reacted to modern technological society. The author, Jacob Neusner, professor of religious studies at Brown University and a prolific scholar of rabbinic Judaism and of Pharisaism in particular, has emerged along with Himmelfarb as one of the most vocal, albeit controversial, interpreters of the current Jewish cultural scene. At times, like Himmelfarb, he has been critical of aspects of American Judaism's traditional liberalism. In the final portion of this volume he tackles the question of whether we are witnessing the last stages of the demise of traditional Judaism or the beginning of a fundamentally new human creation.

Finally, *Jewish Radicalism: A Selected Anthology* edited by Jack Nusan Porter and Peter Dreier (New York, Grove Press, 1973, $7.95) serves as a good introduction to an important Jewish influence upon American society in the last decade. Why the high Jewish participation in the radical movements which some Jews fear will result in an anti-Semitic reaction on the part of the general American populace? Why the widespread disenchantment with religious and cultural aspects of American Judaism by so many of its young people? These are the concrete issues that this book's essays help to clarify. They are important issues for American society generally, and without some grasp of the radical segments of American Judaism the outsider will have a truncated picture of the real-life state of American Judaism today.

ADULT EDUCATION PROGRAM

by Robert Heyer, Jean Marie Hiesberger

GENERAL INTRODUCTION

The purpose of this educational supplement is to provide a practical plan for adult religious education. This plan will be based on selected articles from each issue of NEW CATHOLIC WORLD and will provide adult education programs for eight weeks.

Each session will be built upon key articles and will explode outward from these experiences, information, and group techniques.

The NEW CATHOLIC WORLD ADULT EDUCATION PROGRAM provides:

—continuous preplanned adult education program
—rich range of topics
—short-term commitment
—CCD teacher-enrichment program
—probing content-articles on today's issues integrated with experience-centered educational plans
—educational tools that are practical and spark interest

The creation of a climate conducive to learning is very important. A proper climate in an educational setting should help people be at ease and should stimulate sharing as well as personal activity. Clear, concise directions and careful preparation will facilitate this. Therefore:

—the director should prepare carefully beforehand.
—participants should have read the related articles.

—if a series of directions are given the director should wait until one stage is completed before anouncing the next stage.
—the purpose of each session as well as its relation to the whole should be explained.

I. FIRST WEEK PROGRAM
(90 Minutes)
ROOTS OF ANTI-SEMITISM

A. INTRODUCTION

—The aim of this session is a personal recognition of the evil roots of anti-Semitism as well as its evil in our day.
—Participants should read and have copy of Ruether's article.
—Materials: large newsprint pads and markers for each group. Paper and pencil for each participant.

B. EDUCATIONAL PLAN

1. Director begins by making sure all have articles and paper. (a) Then ask each person in silence to write the words that come to mind when he/she hears the term Jew. (b) Next ask group to turn paper over and complete this sentence: From my experi-

ence (X) I have learned that Jews are (X).

2. Divide into small groups. Time of introductions.
3. The task of each group: Each person presents his "words" that he wrote (cf. la). These should merely be listed on newsprint. Second, share completed sentences (cf. lb). In discussing these, the group should evaluate the relation between the result and the experience.
4. Each small group should be assigned one of the following pages from Ruether's article (12-13, 14, 15, 16, 17). The group should briefly list on newsprint #2 all the laws that are against Jews which occur on their page (e.g., "against building synagogue"). Alongside of each, if possible, list motive for law. Third, list any written or unwritten rules that exist today that discriminate against Jews (or another minority).
5. Small groups present (a) their list of "words"; (b) their analysis of the roots of prejudice. After "a," director should have entire group comment on whether or not there is any implied prejudice in these words. Director might also note any relationships between "b" and "a."
6. Director should conclude by composing with group a list of practical rules for avoiding prejudice.
7. Conclude with coffee and cake.

II. SECOND WEEK PROGRAM
(90 Minutes)
JEWISHNESS OF JESUS

A. INTRODUCTION
—The purpose of this session is to appreciate the difference between external religion and interior religion and to understand that Jesus was fully a Jew.
—Participants should read Suriano's article and have copy at meeting.

B. EDUCATIONAL PLAN
1. Divide participants into small groups. Each group will focus on *one* of the following: (1) Jesus and the Torah; (2) Jesus and the Temple; (3) Jesus and the Pharisees. It would be helpful to designate groups accordingly.
2. The first task of the small group is to share what each member thought about Jesus' attitude toward the Torah, the Temple, or the Pharisees. It would be easier to discuss: Did reading "The Jewishness of Jesus" reveal any false ideas I had about Jesus as a Jew?
3. Each small group should create and prepare role-playing scenario (a concrete event) of Jesus if he were to become man today as a Christian and how he would react to some Christian use of Scripture, Church, or ministry. This should illustrate either the problem of the spirit versus the letter of the law or the temptation to have external religion on Sunday without interior religion.
4. Each group presents #3.
5. Conclude with a prayer for interior religion.

III. THIRD WEEK PROGRAM
(90 Minutes)
UNDERSTAND LITURGICAL ROOTS

A. INTRODUCTION
—The goal of this session is to appreciate that the Eucharistic Cov-

71

enant has its roots in the Jewish Passover.
—Materials: prepare parallel columns of Scripture readings for each person: (a) Exodus 12 and Luke 22:7-12; (b) Deut. 6:2-6 and Mk. 12: 28-34.

B. EDUCATIONAL PLAN

1. Director presents aim and overview of the relationship of Jewish and Christian liturgy.
   An overview sample:
   The Last Supper took place in the context of a paschal meal. In the paschal meal the Jews remembered and relived the experience of the Exodus—their passage from slavery to freedom. Every liturgical detail of the celebration—the clothing worn, the food eaten—was to further the re-creation of the experience of the first exodus. The pasch began with the father praising God for having given this feast to his family and then he carefully explained the meaning of the meal.
   The bread was the bread of affliction, the unleavened bread baked in haste, the sign of having undergone a great suffering. The lamb signified the night of deliverance from Egypt. At the end of the meal, the father took a cup of wine and said a final blessing and prayed for God's mercy on Israel and its people. The Passover meal was a celebration not only of a past event but of the present blessing of being God's people brought out of bondage to freedom, from death to life.
   It was within this context that Jesus chose to explain to his disciples the meaning of the bread and wine, in terms of his own act of deliverance, his own passage from death to life. "This is my body given for you" transformed the meaning and power of the unleavened bread and evoked the reality of a sacrifice which would be present for all time in the person of Jesus. Jesus then took the cup of benediction and said: "This is my covenant blood poured out for you." Now men would celebrate a new passover, the passage of the New Israel, from death to risen life.

2. Divide into small groups.
3. Take time to read Scripture sheets.
4. The task of each group is to examine the Scripture selections for similarities of Covenant and Eucharist to the Jewish Passover-Covenant celebration, and to ask: Is it important to retain these traditions? Why and how do we recall these roots of Covenant and Passover?
5. Sharing of #4.
6. Conclude with prayer based on Mark.

IV. FOURTH WEEK PROGRAM
(90 Minutes)
JEWISH BELIEFS

A. INTRODUCTION
—The aim of this session is to understand and appreciate the creed, code, and cult of the Jewish religion.
—Make necessary preparations for invitation and/or visitation.

B. EDUCATIONAL PLAN
Invite a rabbi to explain the religious creed, code, and cult of Judaism to your group.

This might best be accomplished by visiting his synagogue for your meeting. The rabbi would be more able to present his message and explain the symbols and practices of Judaism.

V. FIFTH WEEK PROGRAM
(90 Minutes)
EDUCATING FOR VALUES

A. INTRODUCTION
—The purpose of this session is to appreciate the religious dimension of educating for values.
—Participants should read Greenberg's article.
—Materials needed: large board or newsprint for entire group and newsprint plus marker for each small group.

B. EDUCATIONAL PLAN
1. Director presents briefly the three dimensions of Jewish religious formation, viz., at home, the study of Scripture, and intellectual comprehension. Also focus on the goal of this session.
2. Have a general brainstorming session. Ask the participants: What are the central expressions of Christian faith that must be taught to children? Write these on board as answers are presented. When board is filled, give some time for participants to reflect and choose the most important item.
3. Divide into small groups. Each group should choose three high-priority statements to teach in the family.
4. The task of each group: discuss (1) how faith differs from blind obedience; (2) what are positive methods of teaching the three

statements of faith to children at home.
5. Groups should summarize best methods on large newsprint.
6. Sharing of small group discussions.
7. General discussion on how the parish can help parents implement this learning process.
8. Conclude with a prayer. Using statements from brainstorming as petitions, with a response of "Lord, help our belief," would be good.

VI. SIXTH WEEK PROGRAM
(90 Minutes)
LEARNING FROM A KIBBUTZ

A. INTRODUCTION
—The aim of this session is to understand how the parish is a community of persons and the purpose and final ways of growing as such.
—Participants should read Lahey's article and have copy at meeting.
—Preparation of two groups of three to present the origin, motivation, strengths and weaknesses in (a) community of people and (b) community of purpose as applied to a kibbutz and the Church.

B. EDUCATIONAL PLAN
1. Director presents briefly the goal and introduces two prepared teams. He might briefly relate concepts of community of purpose and community of people to American Catholic experience. The Catholic school produced a community of purpose; today religious look for community of people.

2. Team A and B present community of people and community of purpose. It would be helpful to present these simultaneously according to origin, motivation, strengths and weaknesses. It would be good if teams could design a visual to help presentation.
3. Participants should have copy of article for consultation during presentation and small group work.
4. Divide into small groups. Select a recorder.
5. The task of small groups is to discuss: (a) How is the parish a community of purpose? (b) How is it a community of persons? (c) In the light of the strengths and weaknesses of these types of community, how can the parish grow into a community of persons with a common purpose of faith?
6. Each group should recommend one significant action that the parish could take in order to achieve this goal.
7. Presentation of #6. These should be presented to effective authority.
8. Conclude with a prayer for community.

VII. SEVENTH WEEK PROGRAM
(90 Minutes)
SHARING RELIGIOUS EXPERIENCE

A. INTRODUCTION
—The aim of this session is to enrich family religious practices by sharing tradition.
—Preparation: Invite several Jewish couples to present ways in which each religiously celebrates and prays at home as a family and in-

dividually. Call rabbi for suggestions of persons to do this. Also several couples from the parish group should prepare to do the same.
—An alternate to this is to study Vatican II's Declaration on the Relationship of the Church to Non-Christian Religions, nn. 4 and 5. Use small groups to discover where these attitudes have not been common and how to develop and implement attitudes based on this belief.

B. EDUCATIONAL PLAN
1. Director introduces the panel members and the goal.
2. Panel presentation of family religious practices. Questions from the group.
3. Divide into small groups. Visitors should join various small groups. The task is to share more the experiences of family prayer, and each group should work out one of their shared experiences of family prayer for presentation to the entire group.
4. Sharing of #3.
5. Coffee and cake.

VIII. EIGHTH WEEK PROGRAM
(90 Minutes)
DESIGNING THE AGENDA

A. INTRODUCTION
—The goal of this session is to appreciate priority commitments of Christian religious community and common possibilities of co-operation.
—Participants should read Tanenbaum's article.
—Materials: Prepare an outline on paper of Tanenbaum's foreign

and domestic agenda.

—Analyze article and list topics of agenda (e.g., Jews in Russia) and motive (e.g., religious freedom). Large newsprint and markers for each small group.

B. EDUCATIONAL PLAN

1. Director introduces session by presenting goal.
2. Divide into small groups. Allow time for introductions and appointing recorder.
3. Task of each small group is to consider: (a) What are the two most important foreign concerns of American Catholics? (b) What are five very important domestic concerns of American Catholics?
4. Each group should make a chart listing the agenda item (foreign and domestic) and the motive for importance of each item.
5. Give out sheet with Tanenbaum's agenda. Small group should compare their own and this.
6. Presentation of small groups' agenda. Note the common elements with Tanenbaum's agenda.
7. Director presents Tanenbaum's suggestion of organizing Catholic-Jewish agenda meetings.
8. Conclude with decision on suggestion.

Guidelines and Suggestions for Implementing the Conciliar Declaration "In Our Time" January 2, 1975

The declaration "Nostra Aetate," issued by the Second Vatican Council on Oct. 28, 1965, "on the relationship of the church to non-Christian "religions" (n. 4), marks an important milestone in the history of Jewish-Christian relations.

Moreover, the step taken by the Council finds its historical setting in circumstances deeply affected by the memory of the persecution and massacre of Jews which took place in Europe just before and during the Second World War.

Although Christianity sprang from Judaism, taking from it certain essential elements of its faith and divine cult, the gap dividing them was deepened more and more, to such an extent that Christian and Jew hardly knew each other.

After 2,000 years, too often marked by mutual ignorance and frequent confrontation, the declaration "Nostra Aetate" provides an opportunity to open or to continue a dialogue with a view to better mutual understanding. Over the past nine years many steps in this direction have been taken in various countries.

As a result it is easier to distinguish the conditions under which a new relationship between Jews and Christians may be worked out and developed. This seems the right moment to propose, following the guidelines of the Council, some concrete suggestions born of experience, hoping that they will help to bring into actual existence in the life of the church the intentions expressed in the conciliar document.

While referring the reader back to this document, we may simply restate here that the spiritual bonds and historical links binding the church to Judaism condemn (as opposed to the very spirit of Christianity) all forms of anti-Semitism and discrimination, which in any case the dignity of the human person alone would suffice to condemn. Further still, these links and relationships render obligatory a better mutual understanding and renewed mutual esteem. On the practical level in particular, Christians must therefore strive to acquire a better knowledge of the basic components of the religious tradition of Judaism; they must strive to learn by what essential traits the Jews define themselves in the light of their own religious experience.

With due respect for such matters of principle, we simply propose some first practical applications in different essential areas of the church's life, with a view to launching or developing sound relations between Catholics and their Jewish brothers.

I. Dialogue

To tell the truth, such relations as there have been between Jew and Christian have scarcely ever risen above the level of monologue. From now on real dialogue must be established.

Dialogue presupposes that each side wishes to know the other, and wishes to increase and deepen its knowledge of the other. It constitutes a particularly suitable means of favoring a better mutual knowledge, and, especially in the case of dialogue between Jews and Christians, of probing the riches of one's own tradition. Dialogue demands respect for the other as he is; above all, respect for his faith and his religious convictions.

In virtue of her divine mission, and her very nature, the church must preach Jesus Christ to the world (Ad Gentes, 2). Lest the witness of Catholics to Jesus Christ should give offense to Jews, they must take care to live and spread their Christian faith while maintaining the strictest respect for religious liberty in line with the teaching of the Second Vatican Council (Declaration "Dignitatis Humanae"). They will likewise strive to understand the difficulties which arise for the Jewish soul—rightly imbued with an extremely high, pure notion of the divine transcendence—when faced with the mystery of the incarnate Word.

While it is true that a widespread air of suspicion, inspired by an unfortunate past, is still dominant in this particular area, Christians, for their part, will be able to see to what extent the responsibility is theirs and deduce practical conclusions for the future.

In addition to friendly talks, competent people will be encouraged to meet and to study together the many problems deriving from the fundamental convictions of Judaism and of Christianity. In order not to hurt (even involuntarily) those taking part, it will be vital to guarantee not only tact but a great openness of spirit and diffidence with respect to one's own prejudices.

In whatever circumstances as shall prove possible and mutually acceptable, one might encourage a common meeting in the presence of God, in prayer and silent meditation, a highly efficacious way of finding that humility, that openness of heart and mind, necessary prerequisites for a deep knowledge of oneself and of others. In particular, that will be done in connection with great causes such as the struggle for peace and justice.

II. Liturgy

The existing links between the Christian liturgy and the Jewish liturgy will be borne in mind. The idea of a living community in the service of God, and in the service of men for the love of God, such as it is realized in the liturgy, is just as characteristic of the Jewish liturgy as it is of the Christian one. To improve Jewish-Christian relations it is important to take cognizance of those common elements of the liturgical life (formulas, feasts, rites, etc.) in which the Bible holds an essential place.

An effort will be made to acquire a better understanding of whatever in the Old Testament retains its own perpetual value (cf. Dei Verbum, 14-15). since that has not been canceled by the later interpretation of the New Testament. Rather, the New Testament brings out the full meaning of the Old, while both Old and New illumine and explain each other. This is all the more important since liturgical reform is now bringing the text of the Old Testament ever more frequently to the attention of Christians.

When commenting on Biblical texts, emphasis will be laid on the continuity of our faith with that of the earlier covenant, in the perspective of the promises, without minimizing those elements of Christianity which are original. We believe that those promises were fulfilled with the first coming of Christ. But it is nonetheless true that we still await their perfect fulfillment in His glorious return at the end of time.

With respect to liturgical readings, care will be taken to see that homilies based on them will not distort their meaning, especially when it is a question of passages which seem to show the Jewish people as such in an unfavorable light. Efforts will be made so

to instruct the Christian people that they will understand the true interpretation of all the texts and their meaning for the contemporary believer.

Commissions entrusted with the task of liturgical translation will pay particular attention to the way in which they express those phrases and passages which Christians, if not well informed, might misunderstand because of prejudice. Obviously, one cannot alter the text of the Bible. The point is that, with a version destined for liturgical use, there should be an overriding preoccupation to bring out explicitly the meaning of a text* while taking scriptural studies into account.

The preceding remarks also apply to introductions to Biblical readings, to the Prayer of the Faithful and to commentaries printed in missals used by the laity.

III. Teaching and Education

Although there is still a great deal of work to be done, a better understanding of Judaism itself and its relationship to Christianity has been achieved in recent years thanks to the teaching of the church, the study and research of scholars, as also to the

---

*Thus the formula "the Jews" in St. John sometimes, according to the context, means "the leaders of the Jews" or "the adversaries of Jesus," terms which express better the thought of the Evangelist and avoid appearing to arraign the Jewish people as such. Another example is the use of the words "Pharisee" and "Pharisaism" which have taken on a largely pejorative meaning.

beginning of dialogue. In this respect, the following facts deserve to be recalled.

¶It is the same God, "inspirer and author of the books of both Testaments" (Dei Verbum, 16), who speaks both in the old and new covenants.

¶Judaism in the time of Christ and the Apostles was a complex reality, embracing many different trends, many spiritual, religious, social and cultural values.

¶The Old Testament and the Jewish tradition founded upon it must not be set against the New Testament in such a way that the former seems to constitute a religion of only justice, fear and legalism, with no appeal to the love of God and neighbor. (cf. Deut. 6:5; Lev. 19:18; Matt. 22: 34-40).

¶Jesus was born of the Jewish people, as were His Apostles and a large number of His first disciples. When He revealed himself as the Messiah and Son of God (cf. Matt 16:16), the bearer of the new Gospel message, He did so as the fulfillment and perfection of the earlier revelation. And although his teaching had a profoundly new character, Christ, nevertheless, in many instances, took His stand on the teaching of the Old Testament. The New Testament is profoundly marked by its relation to the Old. As the Second Vatican Council declared: "God, the inspirer and author of the books of both Testaments, wisely arranged that the New Testament be hidden in the Old and the Old be made manifest in the New" (Dei Verbum, 16). Jesus also used teaching methods similar to those employed by the rabbis of His time.

¶With regard to the trial and death of Jesus, the Council recalled that "what happened in His Passion cannot be blamed upon all the Jews then living, without distinction, nor upon the Jews of today" (Nostra Aetate, 4).

¶The history of Judaism did not end with the destruction of Jerusalem, but rather went on to develop a religious tradition. And although we believe that the importance and meaning of that tradition were deeply affected by the coming of Christ, it is still nonetheless rich in religious values.

¶With the prophets and the Apostle Paul, "the Church awaits the day, known to God alone, on which all peoples will address the Lord in a single voice and 'serve Him with one accord' (Soph. 3:9)" (Nostra Aetate, 4).

Information concerning these questions is important at all levels of Christian instruction and education. Among sources of information, special attention should be paid to the following:

¶Catechisms and religious textbooks.

¶History books.

¶The mass-media (press, radio, cinema, television).

The effective use of these means presupposes the thorough formation of instructors and educators in training schools, seminaries and universities.

Research into the problems bearing on Judaism and Jewish-Christian relations will be encouraged among specialists, particularly in the fields of exegesis, theology, history and sociology. Higher institutions of Catholic research, in association if possible with other similar Christian institutions and experts, are invited to contribute to the solution of such problems. Wherever possible, chairs of Jewish studies will be created and collaboration with Jewish scholars encouraged.

IV. Joint Social Action

Jewish and Christian tradition, founded on the Word of God, is aware of the value of the human person, the image of God. Love of the same God must show itself in effective action for the good of mankind. In the spirit of the prophets, Jews and Christians will work willingly together, seeking social justice and peace at every level—local, national and international.

At the same time, such collaboration can do much to foster mutual understanding and esteem.

Conclusion

The Second Vatican Council has pointed out the path to follow in promoting deep fellowship between Jews and Christians. But there is still a long road ahead.

The problem of Jewish-Christian relations concerns the church as such, since it is when "pondering her own mystery" that she comes up against the mystery of Israel. Therefore, even in areas where no Jewish communities exist, this remains an important problem. There is also an ecumenical aspect to the question: The very return of Christians to the sources and origins of their faith, grafted onto the earlier covenant, helps the search for unity in Christ, the cornerstone.

In this field the bishops will know what best to do on the pastoral level, within the general disciplinary framework of the church and in line with the common teaching of her magisterium. For example, they will create some suitable commissions or secretariats on a national or regional level, or appoint some competent person to promote the implementation of the conciliar directives and the suggestions made above.

On Oct. 22, 1974, the Holy Father instituted for the universal church a commission for religious relations with Judaism, joined to the Secretariat for Promoting Christian Unity. This special commission, created to encourage and foster religious relations between Jews and Catholics— and to do so eventually in collaboration with other Christians—will be, within the limits of its competence, at the service of all interested organizations, providing information for them and helping them to pursue their task in conformity with the instructions of the Holy See.

The commission wishes to develop this collaboration in order to implement, correctly and effectively, the express intentions of the Council.

Declaration on Non-Christian Religions, October 28, 1965

The Jewish Religion

4. As the Council searches into the mystery of the Church, it remembers the spiritual bonds which tie the people of the New Covenant to the offspring of Abraham.

Thus the Church of Christ acknowledges that, according to God's saving design, the beginnings of her faith and her election are found already in the patriarchs, Moses and the prophets. She professes that all who believe in Christ—Abraham's sons according to the faith (cf. Gal. 3, 7)—are included in this patriarch's call, and likewise that the salvation of the Church is symbolically prefigured in the exodus of the chosen people from the land of bondage. The Church, therefore, cannot forget that she received the revelation of the Old Testament through the people with whom God in his inexpressible mercy made the ancient covenant. Nor can she forget that she draws sustenance from the root of that well-cultivated olive tree onto which have been grafted the wild shoots, the Gentiles (cf. Rom. 11, 17-24). Indeed, the Church believes that by his cross Christ, who is our Peace, reconciled Jews and Gentiles, making the two one in himself (cf. Eph. 2, 14-16).

The Church keeps ever in mind the words of the Apostle about his kinsmen: "Theirs is the sonship and the glory and the covenant and the law and the worship and the promises; theirs are the fathers and from them is the Christ according to the flesh" (Rom. 9, 4-5), the Son of the Virgin Mary. She also recalls that the apostles, the Church's foundation-stones and pillars, as well as most of the early disciples who proclaimed the Gospel of Christ to the world, sprang from the Jewish people.

As Holy Scripture testifies, Jerusalem did not recognize the time of her visitation (cf. Luke 19, 44), nor did the Jews, in large number, accept the Gospel; indeed, not a few of them opposed its dissemination (cf. Rom. 11, 28). Nevertheless, now as before, God holds the Jews most dear for the sake of their fathers; he does not repent of the gifts he makes or of the calls he issues—such is the witness of the Apostle (cf. Rom. 11, 28-29). Nevertheless, now as before, God holds the Jews most dear for the sake of their fathers; he does not repent of the gifts he makes or of the calls he issues—such is the witness of the Apostle (cf. Rom. 11, 28-29; also cf. *Dogmatic Constitution on the Church: A.A.S.* 57 [1965], p. 20). In company with the prophets and the same Apostle, the Church awaits that day, known to God alone, on which all peoples will address the Lord with a single voice and "serve him with one accord" (Soph. 3, 9; cf. Is. 66, 23; Ps. 65, 4; Rom. 11, 11-32).

Since the spiritual patrimony common to Christians and Jews is then so rich, the Council wishes to foster and commend mutual understanding and esteem. This will be the fruit, above all, of biblical and theological studies and of brotherly dialogues.

True, the Jewish authorities and those who followed their lead pressed for the death of Christ (cf. John 19, 6); still, what happened in his passion cannot be charged against all the Jews, without distinction, then alive, nor against the Jews of today. Although the Church is the new People of God, the Jews should not be represented as rejected by God or accursed, as if this followed from Holy Scripture. All should see to it, then, that in catechetical work and in the preaching of the Word of God they teach nothing save what conforms to the truth of the Gospel and the spirit of Christ.

The Church, moreover, rejects every persecution against any man. For this reason and for the sake of the patrimony she shares with the Jews, the Church decries hatreds, persecutions and manifestations of anti-Semitism directed against Jews at any time and by anyone. She does so, not impelled by political reasons, but moved by the spiritual love of the Gospel.

Besides, Christ underwent his passion and death freely and out of infinite love because of the sins of men in order that all might reach salvation. This the Church has always taught and teaches still; it is therefore the duty of the Church to proclaim the cross of Christ as the sign of God's all-embracing love and as the fountain from which every grace flows.

Universal Brotherhood, Excluding Every Discrimination

5. We cannot truly call upon God, the Father of all, if we refuse to treat in a brotherly way any class of men, created as all are in the image of God. Man's relation to God, the Father, and his relation to men, his brothers, are so linked together that Scripture says: "He who does not love does not know God" (1 John 4, 8).

No foundation therefore remains for any theory or practice that leads to discrimination between man and man or people and people insofar as their human dignity and the rights flowing from it are concerned.

The Church reproves, as foreign to the mind of Christ, any discrimination against men or harassment of them because of their race, color, condition in life or religion. On the contrary, following the footsteps of the holy apostles Peter and Paul, the Council ardently implores the Christian faithful to "maintain good fellowship aming the nations" (1 Pet. 2, 12) and, if possible, to live for their part in peace with all men (cf. Rom. 12, 18), so that they may truly be sons of the Father who is in heaven (cf. Matt. 5, 45).

Commentary
John B. Sheerin, C.S.P.

Two and a half million Jews surrounded by one hundred million Arabs: this is the plight of the Israelis in the Middle East today. To be surrounded by unfriendly neighbors is no new experience for the Jewish people. For long centuries in Christian Europe, small colonies of Jews were surrounded by vast Christian populations who launched raids into Jewish quarters of big cities, harassing Jews or humiliating them by stripping them of basic human rights and decencies. Why? Largely because of a widespread misunderstanding of the Gospel and horror fables about a curse God was said to have inflicted on the Jews for their part in the Crucifixion.

Pope John, elected to the papacy in 1958, resolved to put a stop to this distortion of Christianity by creating a new climate of understanding between Catholics and Jews. As papal representative in Istanbul he had come to know Jews intimately and to help them considerably. His first step was to ask Cardinal Bea to prepare for the approval of the forthcoming Second Vatican Council a declaration of sympathetic understanding of the Jewish people. After a long-drawn-out crossfire of controversy on the Council floor, some behind-the-scenes maneuvering, strong Arab pressures and extensive revising of the draft document, the final text of the statement on the Jews was ap-

proved by the Bishops, 2221 in favor as against 88 opposed. The statement was promulgated by Pope Paul on October 28, 1965 as part of a larger document titled *Declaration on the Relation of the Church to Non-Christian Religions* (which included Hinduism, Buddhism and Islam.)

The statement on the Jews was warmly greeted by most Catholics (perhaps because they had not actually read the text which contained items that would certainly give them a jolt). In the text, the Bishops acknowledged that the Old Testament came to us from the Jews, that the Christian religion was nourished by the Jewish religion, that Jesus, Mary and Joseph were Jews and most important of all, that God still loves the Jewish people as his chosen. "Nevertheless, now as before, God holds the Jews most dear for the sake of their fathers: he does not repent of the gifts he makes or the calls he issues—such is the witness of the Apostle (cf. Rom. 11, 28-29.)" We used to say that we admired the religion of ancient Israel but not modern Judaism (which was equivalent to saying that the only good Jews are dead Jews). But here was the Second Vatican Council asserting that God has not rejected the Jewish people, since God never revokes his calls or his gifts, and supporting the claim by a text from St. Paul.

The text went on to state that the

Jewish people cannot be charged collectively with the killing of Christ. "What happened in his Passion cannot be charged against all Jews, without distinction, then alive, nor against the Jews of today." Therefore, the Bishops demanded that Catholics should never represent Jews as "rejected by God or accursed" and that all teachers and preachers should be careful to teach only "what conforms to the truth of the Gospel and the spirit of Christ." The Church, moreover, rejects every persecution and in stating this point, the Bishops broaden their horizon in the concluding paragraph of the text and strike at violations of human dignity anywhere. "The Church reproves, as foreign to the mind of Christ, any discrimination against men or harassment of them because of their race, color, condition in life or religion."

Some American Jews were critical not of the document itself (whose merits they acknowledged) but of the deletion of terms that appeared in early drafts of the document but not in the final text. It is true that there were deletions but it would be hard to prove that these omissions were done deliberately to water down the text. It seems quite plausible that certain deletions were made to help win as many votes as possible for the text without corrupting it. A Council document that is not backed by an overwhelming consensus would be very hard to implement. A 5-4 U.S. Supreme Court decision represents a wide-open split in the mind of the Court and is hard to enforce: the public feels that if the same issue comes up again before the Court, it might easily decide 5-4 in the other direction. So the Bishops worked toward as high a consensus as possible for the Jewish statement.

Surprisingly, the deletion that most alarmed the Jews, both here and abroad, was the omission of the word "deicide" that appeared in an earlier draft but was absent from the final text. Most Americans at the Council were not familiar with the word but apparently it had been frequently used by anti-Semites in Europe to launch pogroms. It meant the crime of killing God. An early draft had it that "the Jewish people never should be represented as accursed or guilty of deicide." The final text had ". . . as rejected by God or accursed." Some Council experts admitted the word "deicide" was "ugly" and should be completely excised from the Christian vocabulary but considered it an absurd term: God cannot be killed, and certainly Jews could not be guilty of deicide in killing one they did not consider divine. It was all a tempest in a philological teapot.

Another deleted word was "condemns." An early draft said, "The Church . . . decries and condemns hatreds and persecutions directed against Jews" but the final text omitted "condemns." This deletion set off explosions at the Council in spite of the fact that Pope John, fed up with papal and Conciliar condemnations, had asked the Bishops at the beginning of the Council not to condemn anything but simply apply the medicine of mercy to evils. American Jews however welcomed the insertion of the word "anti-Semitism" into the above sentence, i.e., "The Church decries hatreds, persecutions and manifestations of anti-Semitism directed against Jews at any time by anyone." Probably all Jews took special note of the fact that it was a German, Cardinal Bea, who focused a heavy emphasis on "the violent and criminal" anti-Semitism in his own country that had caused the deaths of millions of Jews.

The Catholic-Jewish dialogue made substantial progress immediately after the Council but came to an abrupt halt at the time of the six-day war in 1967. When it looked as though Soviet Russia might intervene on the side of the Arabs to carry out Arab threats to exterminate the Israelis, American Jews looked to Christians for an expression of human concern for the plight of the Israelis. The top Catholic and Protestant officials in America were silent, the dialogue ended. "You were silent when the six million were murdered in Germany: now you are silent again when another slaughter is threatened." However the dialogue gradually picked up momentum in the United States, aided by a fine set of guidelines issued by the American Bishops' Catholic-Jewish Secretariat. This document reassured the Jews and helped clear the atmosphere. They stated for instance that proselytizing must be avoided in dialogue, that the Crucifixion story must not be so presented as to involve the Jews in collective guilt, that Catholic scholars are urged to acknowledge the permanent election of the Jewish people as a chosen people.

In November, 1969 a working document, designed to bring about fuller implementation of the Council document, was made public by Cardinal Shehan of Baltimore. It carried the main themes of the Council text to new levels of ecumenical awareness, adding a few welcome items and emphases. It urged Christians to see the Jews as they see themselves—a people with whom God made a covenant, joining to the covenant a gift of land which has endured in the Jewish soul as a continuing object of aspiration. "The existence of the state of Israel should not be separated from this perspective . . ." This working document (not yet a final text) stated that "all intent of proselytizing and conversion" must be excluded from the dialogue, that homilists should take special care in correctly interpreting Bible readings "especially of those which seem to put the Jewish people in an unfavorable light." It also asked that commissions in charge of liturgical translations give special attention to passages which can be interpreted by uninformed Christians "in a tendentious fashion." It cited in particular the rendering of St. John's references to "the Jews" and various Gospel references to "the Pharisees" which have acquired a pejorative coloring.

Apparently this working document passed through several revisions before a new set of guidelines was released on January 2, 1975: Pope Paul had created a new *Commission for Religious Relations with the Jews* on October 22, 1974. The new Commission is joined to the Secretariat for Promoting Christian Unity. Father

Edward Flannery, director of the American Bishops' Catholic-Jewish Secretariat, has praised the new guidelines while expressing regret for the omission of any reference to the state of Israel or to proselytizing in dialogue. Rabbi Marc Tanenbaum of the American Jewish Committee also praised the document but was unhappy about a strong emphasis on the Church's right to evangelize contained in the text. He felt that talk of conversion in a set of guidelines for dialogue "cannot but cast doubt on the motivation of the entire program."

The new document calls for shared prayer between Christians and Jews, points up the responsibility of striving to learn how the Jews define themselves in the light of their own religious experience, urges Christians to take cognizance of the common elements in Christian and Jewish liturgical life as well as the basic Jewishness of Christ, the Apostles and Gospel teaching. It reiterates with a sense of urgency the demands of the 1960 working document for caution and care on the part of homilists lest they show the Jews as such in an unfavorable light: it also echoes the 1969 text's plea to commissions entrusted with the task of liturgical translation "to pay particular attention to the way in which they express those phrases and passages which Christians, if not well informed, might misunderstand because of prejudice." The text repeats also the 1969 document's references to "the Jews" and to "the Pharisees." Strangely the text says that Christians "must strive to learn by what essential traits the Jews define themselves in the light of their own religious experience" yet makes no reference whatever to Israel. The most dramatic trait of Jewish religion is the deep-felt bond between the Jewish people and the land God gave them at the time of the covenant, the holy land they see in the perspective of their attachment to Jerusalem.

Aside from the omission of any reference to Israel or to the proselytizing problem, the new guidelines are a welcome step forward in Catholic-Jewish relations. The new Vatican Committee, headed by Cardinal Willebrands, a long-time friend of the Jews, seems to mean business and its tone is hopeful and confident. So be it. One holocaust this century is enough.